THE BOOK OF JONAH

THE BOOK OF JONAH

Jonah Barrington
with Clive Everton

STANLEY PAUL / LONDON

STANLEY PAUL & CO LTD
3 Fitzroy Square, London W1

AN IMPRINT OF THE HUTCHINSON GROUP

London Melbourne Sydney Auckland
Wellington Johannesburg Cape Town
and agencies throughout the world

First published 1972

This book has been set in Baskerville type, printed in Great Britain
on antique wove paper by Anchor Press, and
bound by Wm. Brendon, both of Tiptree, Essex

ISBN 0 09 113610 5

Contents

Illustrations

Will his name be John
Or will his name be Jonah
Crying to repent
On the Island of Iona?

Will his name be Jason
Looking for a seaman
Or a mad crusader
Without rhyme or reason?

Louis MacNeice, *Prognosis*

I

First Impressions

Clive Everton

The Book of Jonah was not written by Jonah Barrington (because he did not have the time) nor by an anonymous ghost writer (because he didn't want to be the recipient of praise or blame for something which was not his own work). The larger part of the book consists of an edited transcript of a series of tape recordings. These have not been heavily edited since Jonah epitomises the characteristic Irish ability to talk fluently, coherently and at great length with virtually total recall.

The other chapters were written by me, not as a strictly impartial journalist in the accepted sense but by one who is certainly impartial in the sense that no man is a hero to his valet.

I am not Jonah's valet but, as is related elsewhere, I became professionally associated with him in February 1969 when he turned professional. This everyday contact has inevitably revealed facets of his personality which the public do not normally see. Some people have found certain of these facets not wholly admirable: certain readers may not.

Jonah is obsessively egotistical; years afterwards, he does not easily forgive those who have wounded him; he has impenetrably black depressions in which he is prone, on the most trivial pretext, to hurt those who are nearest to him.

Taken in isolation, none of these characteristics is particularly endearing. Yet in the belief that a man's faults often give the greater validity to his virtues, the intention of the book is to present the real man and no glossy authorised version.

Jonah Barrington is star quality. He behaves like a star and expects to be treated like a star. He has the star's total self-absorbtion. He regards himself as the centre of the universe.

He is also immensely likable, infectiously enthusiastic; outspokenly critical yet, like an impish ten-year-old, possessing—and confident of possessing—an innate charm which gives him access to an inexhaustible fund of goodwill on which he can draw at will to re-establish himself in the good graces of those he has ruffled.

His star quality is hard to define but easy to recognise, a status founded on a high level of achievement but insupportable by achievement alone.

His record stamps him as a great squash player but what distinguishes him from his great predecessors is a drive and personality which has altered and extended the squash world.

His obsessively egotistical desire to prove himself the world's best player goes in harness with the power to analyse clear-headedly and objectively the lines on which the future of squash should develop. While many squash champions have striven to become the biggest fish in the pool, Jonah badly wants the pool to be much bigger.

Historically, he has been fortunate in that the game has begun to grow internationally—notably in the introduction of world team and individual championships—concurrently with the arousal of his own squash ambitions.

But it was not growing fast enough and Jonah's role in accelerating certain aspects of its growth is analogous to the role Joe Davis played in the development of snooker.

Snooker was regarded by the professionals in the mid-twenties, the golden age of billiards, as merely a means of providing some light-hearted knockabout if a billiards session finished early. Davis developed the technique of the game and publicised it to such an extent that it has long since outdistanced billiards in popularity.

Technically, Barrington is not an innovator, except perhaps in establishing the overriding importance of fitness and agility, but he shares Davis's gifts as a publicist and his ability to grow with his chosen game during its most explosive period.

Sales of squash rackets in Britain have trebled in the last ten years but the game is only just beginning to shake off its aura of social exclusiveness. A few squash centres, notably those attached to ABC cinemas, have appeared recently but courts are still located mainly in private clubs, public schools and universities. Some of the wealthier works-sports social clubs possess squash courts but it is executives rather than shop-floor workers who use them.

There are radical differences from this situation in Australia, the country of the present world champions. Almost all courts there are commercially owned and commercially run to make a profit. They are available for hiring by the hour or half-hour by any member of the public. Few courts have a licence to sell drink so the long established British tradition of taking alcoholic refreshment on the premises after violent exercise cannot be perpetuated. Australians are less bothered by this than the British are, for their sport tends to be a self-sufficient activity which does not have to be sustained by a quasi-social setting.

The British ideals of club life emphasise sociability and tend to attempt to smooth the rough edges which are inevitably to be found in the completely dedicated player.

Barrington's dedication is generally admired, albeit grudgingly by some, but it is precisely his dedication and ambition—for the game as well as himself—which has led to many at the soft centre of squash to resent his attempts to place the game fairly and squarely in the public eye and not allow it to remain in the cosy, close-knit and easily controlled world which has always been its oyster.

Ambition and a burning will to win are qualities often taken for granted in Australia. Similar qualities in British players often invite social distrust. Sociability in the bar, conventional modesty, conventional social graces, conventional relegation of sport into a means of relaxation rather than a means of giving life an added purpose or active force—ideals which one could accept from those with no pretensions to sporting achievement—are carried over all too often in British sport to those who participate above county level.

The player of limited ability and potential, who nevertheless wants to realise every scrap of potential that he has, even if this still leaves him well below international standard, is subtly discouraged from doing so by the pervading climate of sociability.

Natural ability, all too often unsupported by a determined mental attitude, is nevertheless usually more highly prized than more pedestrian natural talents even when they are allied to great efforts in training and practice.

The typically British admiration of effortless amateur accomplishment is of course a relic of the phoney amateur ideals transmitted through a recognisable old school tie ethos.

Barrington was educated at Cheltenham College and loathed it with all the vehemence expressed in Lindsay Anderson's film 'If . . .' which, ironically, was shot there. Since then, his life-style, from his instinctive questioning of established authority to the infrequency of his haircuts, has rejected the conventional virtues.

He drinks only when he is thirsty, he makes clear realistic assessments which are uncluttered by false humility or observance of an imagined obligation to feed the self-regard of others.

He is an unrelenting yet generous opponent; an assiduous opener of doors for anonymous old ladies; a bitter denouncer of the Old Pals Act; a more thoughtful and loving son than most who devote a great deal of time and fuss to it; no respecter of persons; and an infinite respecter of persons.

He never takes people at their own valuation but his friendship, when he gives it, is as total and absolute as the loyalty and effort he demands from those he works with. Those who are only 99% with him are against him.

The purpose of our first meeting in early January 1968 gave no indication of the degree to which we would later be associated. Jonah had just won the Open and Amateur and David Talbot, Sports Editor of the *Birmingham Post*, commissioned a 1,000-word feature on squash's recent notable expansion, as exemplified by this interesting young player who had come from nowhere to win the game's two major titles.

We met, as arranged, at the Lansdowne Club at 1.30 where he plied me with salad and yoghourt. I found it difficult to eat, however, because, as soon as we had sat down, he began to talk, or rather to declaim, so coherently, so infinitely quotably, that I was frightened to miss a word.

The interview ended almost four hours later when Jonah's practice opponent arrived. My writing hand was nearly dropping off with the fatigue of amassing a mountain of notes from which I had to distil the essence of this hypnotic young man, who was brimming over with life and humour yet dominated by a puritanical outlook on squash which, at the same time, was a kind of social criticism.

'The sort of thing one sees far too much of in British squash is a good player beating a youngster and going into the bar to knock back pint after pint and make a great thing about never bothering with any proper training. This is a bad influence for a young player and I am determined to knock this kind of person off the top.

'These are empty people. They are the sort of people who say when they are 40: "I could have been amateur champion, you know. I had the natural ability but I had to make a living, etc. etc. . . ."

'I don't want to be one of those people. They are the most boring and empty people in existence. They have a strong sense of failure.

'They are too frightened to take a risk. They have this fear of displaying their struggles in front of everybody and failing. They can't contemplate the possibility of people saying "Look how he's tried everything and *still* he hasn't made it."

'I have always wanted to be a professional sportsman and to be the best in a particular sport. If I fail, I want at least to have the satisfaction of knowing that I have tried everything possible.

'The practice is usually so much drudgery. One is tired; one hasn't recovered from the training the day before. But you must force yourself. You must practise with maximum discipline. The satisfaction comes when you play a good match and you know it's *because* of what you have done.

'In an individual game you must be rather selfish. The better you are, the more selfish you become. Every champion is a very selfish man. Your whole way of life is regulated by the sport.'

2

In the Beginning—1941

Jonah Barrington

I was the youngest member of the family, the third child. I had a sister, Geraldine, who was five years older than me, and a brother, Nick, who was two years older than me, and with whom I was always in competition. I refused to go to bed before him—I couldn't, I mustn't go to bed before him; in the end my parents accepted this and we always went to bed at the same time.

I was always fascinated by sport and played as many sports as I could before I went away to school. These sports were mainly soccer (this was North Cornwall where there was very little Rugby; in fact, I never saw a rugby match until I was forcibly taken to see one at the age of nine when I went to school in Ireland) and some cricket. We used to play cricket on the lawn at home. My brother and I were constantly battling with Tony and David Tape, two friends of ours from a farm just down the road—in two-a-side matches which my brother would always have to win. If he didn't win, he'd usually hit someone.

So many games that we played ended in an out-and-out bashing of junior by senior. The perpetual sense of competition and my memories of the early years of schooling in the village school at Morwenstowe until I was nine years old made this a fantastically happy time.

After that was less satisfactory for a number of reasons: having been brought up so far away from cities and civilisation, we were allowed to run fairly wild. I wouldn't say my parents were terribly strict; they were always firm over certain things but we were allowed tremendous freedom. It was a country life. We were brought up in the country atmosphere surrounded by animals—dogs, hens and pigs, which we kept ourselves—fields and farms. We were also only three-quarters of a mile away from the sea—which doesn't explain why I'm almost totally unable to swim.

We could see the sea, the Atlantic, from the house and at night could hear the roar of the surf. I suppose I was so familiar with it at that time that I didn't appreciate the magnificence of the cliffs along that coast line, but it was a life far removed from the rush and competitive aspect of the city life I lived in London and the life I lead now.

While I don't want to live the life of a recluse I think it would be rather fun to be such a person for about 2½ days and no more. But my desire is not to be involved in business affairs. I find that the routine and hurly-burly of business is something that will remain always foreign to me. It is such a relief to get away from London particularly, and go to the West Country. I'm obviously now not so lazy in my approach as I was seven years ago, but the relaxation that I never get here does come when I go out to that part of the world—because this is my home, Cornwall, North Cornwall: this is where I am best known and where I don't have to compete, somewhere I can return to and feel totally at ease.

My father was a military man and after the second world war he was retired. In fact, he was very retired. He got up at noon and he also used to go to bed very late. He was severe in his approach. He was certainly not a dictator but he was very much in charge. He dominated the evenings, whereas my mother dominated the mornings when my father hadn't risen from his bed—could I be a chip off the old block?

My mother could be very sharp and as I tend to wake up rather slowly, I certainly wasn't in a position to battle for the honour of being top worm-catcher.

But my father was not a sportsman as I am. He was a much more traditional type of sportsman from what we would call the old days; his loves had been shooting, fishing and riding, although it was his boast that he had played for this team or that.

I didn't believe him really for he was prone to exaggerate in certain matters when my brother and I started to have a small degree of success in sports. It was amazing how in his mind my father's ability developed as we grew better and how especially good he had been at this or that sporting enterprise.

My father was a very small man and my brother is very tall. He rapidly outstripped my father in proportion. My father was only about 5′ 7″ and like many small men—Napoleon and others—he did like to assert himself. This he was well able to do since he had a monstrously vile temper which certainly frightened the wits out of us—his children—on many occasions. He was a fighting man; he had an armoury of weapons; he liked guns. He fought in the first world war and the Irish Civil War, and he had a few scars to show that he hadn't been entirely a pacifist.

Had my father been a competitive sportsman, he would have been a killer; he would have been the worst and best type of sportsman. He hated losing and he definitely had a very tough, hard streak. I feel that I'm fortunate to have a certain measure of that streak in myself.

I'm fortunate also in a way that my father was far cleverer than his children. He had an excellent brain which he developed for his own personal satisfaction. He had a sensitive feeling for history and was a great conversationalist. Again and again, I hear old friends say: 'Your father was wonderful in conversation.'

He loved talking; some people would call it a form of compulsive verbal diarrhoea, but whereas in others it could be called this, with him there was always something of interest to be heard. He had a powerful memory, almost photographic. He read ferociously every day of his life. He read in bed and was tremendously interested in anything that could be called antiquity. People say to me that I have no trouble in talking and that this comes quite easily to me. It is obviously something I must have inherited to a certain degree from him and also from my mother because she also is able to tell a tale or two.

But my chief good fortune lay in being the second son with a brother who was reasonably intelligent, so academically set a fair standard, and who also had a certain talent for playing sports. So I found that I was always wanting to compete on his level. This was a struggle but helped me to accept the fact that a lot of things were going to be hard. It was hard to battle with my brother because he was two years older. There's a hell of a difference when one is 9 and the other 11 or 13 and 15.

This feeling of always being the underdog I knew from an early age. I knew what it was to compete, to work, and not to be on top, to struggle and strive to get on the same footing. This has been borne out in this sport. I played because, at the beginning, I was fairly wretched. In fact, the strange thing is that my brother's best sport was squash. He was one of the best schoolboys in Britain and of all the sports we played, I made least impression on him on the squash court. Naturally I thought squash was the worst game that had ever been invented. I much preferred to take him on at table tennis and tennis where I was able to do much better.

Squash is a much more physical game and anything physical at that time I found almost impossible—but not that impossible that I didn't have a go.

And so I have always been prepared to have a go on this basis: this is the influence of those early years. If he passed his examination I felt that I had to pass mine. Out of self-respect one makes the effort, and even though one doesn't appreciate it at that age, it is a habit that forms. Obviously there is an obstinate streak which doesn't allow one to give in. It's great to have this obstinacy although at the time there is little realisation that this is going to play such an important part later on.

When I told my parents I wanted to be a professional footballer, this was very much frowned upon because my father was certainly not from a school which believed in professionalism, particularly as at that time a professional footballer's social standing was poor in relation to the professions and other 'good, decent' jobs. So, to infuriate him, which certainly wasn't difficult, I only had to say I wanted to be a professional sportsman and he would blow his top. The funny thing is that I am a professional sportsman.

I was at school in Ireland for about five years at Headfort Preparatory School in Co. Meath near Kells. I was initially resentful of being sent away from my friends at home—and away from home. This is a bit of a blow at the age of nine. However much you may fight with your family, you don't want to leave home at that time.

I then had an appendix operation within two weeks of my arrival at the school. A cunning move! A typical Barrington ploy which cut the term short by about three weeks in all and allowed me to go on a holiday to recover from the ailment.

As a kid I was a great believer in dirty rhymes and my village school background, the best schooling of my life, prepared me well in that particular department, so much so that during my first year at my prep school I managed to delight the boys of my dormitory with my 'rude' poetry. Regrettably, one night, the headmaster, in the course of his duties, came trotting along the corridor and happened to listen in on my discourse of the night which was, I think, 'Old Mother Riley had a cow' (anon). Whereupon he dug me out of the dormitory, took me down and gave me a mighty beating, six very vicious strokes with the cane.

The stick seemed to be about six feet wide. I will always remember, the following day, the other boys were beaten as well for having enjoyed this particular poetic feast. The headmaster had told me to come along again. I came in at the end of the line, marched in, bent over, and said to him 'How many this time?'—I was treated with mercy.

I had an arch-enemy there named Tregoning, who on one occasion was playing a game of cards with some other boys. The headmaster had joined in. The game certainly wasn't poker, more probably 'Old Maid' or something like that, but in the course of events the said Tregoning lost his particular round, lost the game and came out smartly with a rude Irish word.

The headmaster asked Tregoning what he'd said, and Tregoning said it was something that Barrington minor taught him. So the headmaster went off to the Irish master, who, slightly red faced, gave him the translation—which was roughly 'kiss me arse'.

Whereupon I was called into the headmaster's study to explain myself and given a dreadful warning of final retribution of having to leave the school if that sort of thing continued. And where had I learnt such language? Whereupon I boldly told him that 'my Daddy' had taught me.

'My Daddy' had a letter from the headmaster shortly after that. My father was quite proud of me secretly although in front of mother he pretended he was annoyed. It certainly never stopped his Irish instruction; he always continued his liberal education on such matters; but it did mean that the headmaster looked on me as some kind of sexual prodigy. Whether it was anything to do with my sex education or not, I was always considered to be far more advanced in this than my contemporaries, so that when I left, the headmaster didn't think it worthwhile to give me the traditional talk about sex. I think he thought that I probably knew it all anyway and had done so ever since first cracking a grin in my cradle.

Once I adjusted this was certainly a marvellous period in my life. Headfort was an excellent school, again in the country, on a very large estate, and with the most sympathetic teaching I have ever encountered. I owe a great deal to this school because, strangely enough, there was a squash court there. I probably played my first game of squash when I was about 11 years old but really I don't remember. I think I might have just hit a black ball on the court with a friend of mine. It was, at that time, the only school in Ireland with a squash court.

I was greatly influenced during my schooldays in Meath by the sportsmaster, Jack Sweetman, who had been an Irish rugby trialist several times.

He married a delightful girl, Edith, who was the matron there and they now have a son, Alan, who has been at Headfort and is showing great promise.

Jack Sweetman was really a splendid man. I always think if one really likes a master, one reacts to this and tries to do one's utmost to please and impress. Jack Sweetman I liked for many reasons. He had been a magnificent Rugby player. He was reserve for Ireland on a number of occasions but it was during the McCarthy–McKay Triple Crown period and he was unlucky that he played for an unfashionable club, Old Wesley.

But he was a master thinker, a gentleman and a sportsman. He certainly couldn't have been capable of doing anything really dirty on the rugger pitch. He was an excellent cricketer, who played for Leinster, the inter-provincial side, on God knows how many occasions and he also played for SwindonTown Reserves in the Football Combination at soccer.

When he realised that my feelings were much more for soccer than rugby he was always prepared to encourage me. I think that he would have quite liked to have seen me go on to a soccer rather than a rugby school. But because he was the man he was, eternally helpful and patient, I did my utmost to learn how to play rugby. In the end, I captained the rugby team at the school and looked as though I might become a reasonably proficient player.

I think he was quite enthusiastic about my progress at that stage. I was a tiny fellow, very, very small, but at the age of twelve or thirteen, playing with twelve or thirteen year olds, I was still able to hold my own and more besides; whereas later on, at Cheltenham, when I had to play against fifteen and sixteen year olds, I found that my size was a terrible disadvantage. I was buried pretty rapidly by that school and began to lose enthusiasm for just about everything.

Jack was neither a drinker nor a smoker and you can trace a lot of the elements which have been part of my existence over the last seven years back to him. I always feel that he must have been a bit disappointed in my lack of progress at Cheltenham, and then, afterwards, at Dublin University. I think that it gives him an enormous satisfaction now that I have been able to come through to be a success in this field. He was also my history and geography teacher, and some might say these are more important than sport, but my world is the sport's world. However, he certainly developed in me the love and feeling for history that my father had and I found geography more interesting under him than under anyone else.

I then came into the dark stage of my school career because I did not enjoy my schooling at Cheltenham College, to which I went at the age of thirteen and a half.

I feel that thirteen to seventeen is a decisive period of a boy's life. These are the truly formative years; this is when one is growing from a child into a man, when all the problems and emotional difficulties one is beset by can easily be turned from molehills into mountains by unsympathetic surroundings; and I felt that this type of school was totally unsympathetic.

To me it's a hangover from the Victorian period, an insensitive battery-system producing the 'splendid fellows' sent out to control the British Empire, and inevitably reaping a painful rebound, a boomerang that has caused this country little but discomfort in the last fifteen to twenty years.

I don't feel that this is the sort of school geared to making the right future for a country like Britain. I loathed it.

I feel a measure of this was the fault of the school and some my own, because I had been outstanding in my prep school and now became a totally anonymous figure amongst 450 boys. I think there were about 60 boys at my prep school, and from being a kingpin at one to nothing at the other, created an almost inevitable reaction—the ego suffered!

My reaction was to withdraw into myself and become very rebellious. I despised discipline and fought against it throughout my career at Cheltenham.

My school standards fell away.

Whereas I had shown at Headfort a capacity for application,

at Cheltenham I showed the very opposite and refused to set myself any task at all that would in any sense stretch my powers. I tried to take the easy way out.

The school naturally resented this and I forfeited my rightful place, out of obstinacy on my own part and a certain lack of flexibility in the curriculum of the school and the way that particular curriculum was carried out.

I didn't like the discipline. It is probably inherent in most of us to resent discipline, but even more so I felt that I wasn't given the right sort of opportunity in the sporting field there. This love I have for playing sport is so considerable that I became even then very depressed when things were not going well because, as a youth, I was emotional and my life revolved to a great extent around sport.

I had been very successful at sport and now the competition was that much greater. Because I was a particularly small boy I was at a decided disadvantage. Rugby was the main game at Cheltenham and I made no impression.

I was also going through the stage when my eyesight was starting to fail. I became short-sighted when I was fourteen. I didn't know what was happening to me when I looked at the blackboard and couldn't see the writing on the board. All these emotional difficulties boiled over at once, so much so that at the age of fourteen I had a nervous breakdown.

I had to go away from Cheltenham for part of one term and was sent to some people called Forbes-Dennis at St. Ives. He was a psychologist and philosopher who had been a pupil of Alfred Adler. He and his wife, Phyllis Bottome, the novelist, looked after me for a while. He was very kind and used to listen to me, asking me about my dreams of the night before. I used to make up anything that came into my head and he would try to explain things to me. It was quite funny because I was tricking him, but he was probably tricking me! He must have been helpful as I didn't have any further problem in that way later on.

I had an abiding hatred for the cadet force. Perhaps I wanted to be Napoleon and didn't want to start in the ranks. I wasn't a conscientious objector but I objected to being shunted into a uniform and ordered around.

I think that little things, which might be termed trivial, got on top of me. I thought that uniform was barbaric. I have always been unable to wear anything of a rough cloth and I don't think you'll find anything rougher, for some inexplicable reason, than that battle-dress.

I used to go through this business of wearing pyjamas underneath thinking how soft I must be to have to do this—only to realise that about half the school did the same—but I never found out till afterwards. I must confess that it was bloody hot in the summer sometimes—hot enough in that battle-dress, let alone having those pyjamas on underneath.

Maybe it was a little unfortunate that I had an elder brother there before me, a respectable figure, a splendid figure, a conservative figure and certainly always the white sheep of the family. This doesn't mean that he hasn't the devil in him but it has always been fairly well disguised. I was possessed by the devil, too frequently, while he was a different type of character altogether. He was reassured by conventional standards and has always taken a much more conservative approach to things. I think he is appalled by some of my activities especially as he is now a pillar of the law; but I suppose that what I am doing now is the chain reaction from my resentment of Cheltenham College.

I think this was inevitable reaction because I was fairly successful at my prep school and wanted that success to continue. I like being successful. I loathe any sort of failure. I don't like being second-best. I want to be the best the whole time. It is an instinctive competitive flair and it can cause a considerable amount of emotional suffering, but this was a constant theme throughout my childhood.

There must be many features within that type of structure which are excellent but I felt that there should have been communication between the sexes at that age. Surely this monk-like isolation can only do harm and breed the wrong type of instinct in boys. I think it is much more natural for them to be given every chance to mix with girls so that they don't feel inhibited, nervous or green at seventeen or eighteen when they go into the outside world. I know that I certainly felt very unsure of myself when I left Cheltenham. I'd never had any real contact with girls except that I was fortunate to have a sister to whom I was very close. Even though she was five years older than me I think she was closer to me than my brother simply because I was the baby of the family. Geraldine and my brother Nick used to fight over me and, having stirred it all up, I used to sit back and watch it happening, which was very good because she always came to me for sympathy!

I don't think many other boys really shared my resentment for the school. There was a great emphasis on sport and a successful sportsman found that there were many doors open to him and that he would be richly rewarded and honoured.

As I was not so successful at sport—between the ones that couldn't play at all and the ones who *were* successful—I found that I threw in my lot with those who were not. I had a study with a boy who was intensely interested in the army—he always kept his uniform and boots immaculate—but who just couldn't function on the games field. I felt immense sympathy for him because little opportunity was given for advancement to those who were unable to do well at sport.

I felt a sense of injustice not only towards me but towards those who were particularly good in other spheres, poetry or singing perhaps, which are accomplishments of so much more value and permanence than the ability to pummel one's way into and out of a scrum.

At Cheltenham, I didn't form any friendships at all. I had a number of friends from my prep school days, and when I met up with these at university again it was as if I had never been away, although I hadn't seen them for about five years.

There was an instinctive feeling for them which had always been there whereas I had no lasting friends from my public school. There was no one of whom I could say, 'He was my best friend and I was his best friend.'

I was a little bit of a loner because my instinct when things go wrong is to draw into myself. I loathed that period of my life.

I went to Trinity College, Dublin, because many members of my family had been to Trinity before me. My father didn't in fact go there although he had the opportunity and undoubtedly would have done very well.

He wanted me at one time to go on to another Irish school after Headfort and was quite adamant that Trinity should come after my schooling.

It was his decision and it was one that I leapt at. I was prepared to go anywhere to get away from Cheltenham at the age of 17. My mother would have preferred me to stay at Cheltenham a little longer but the school wasn't very interested in having me and she received a letter saying that it would benefit neither the school nor me if I were to remain there.

She didn't like that at all, but I was determined that I wasn't going to go back to school, and I set off for Trinity about two and a half months later, in October, to study law.

I was interested in the law because there's a certain glamour to it. It wasn't a very practical approach. I was very interested in the major cases and the tremendous oratory of Q.C.'s like Birkett and Carson, who were able to swing the trial round on perhaps just one crucial point.

I could see myself wearing a wig and cutting quite a heroic figure—failing to realise that one would have to go through all the less heroic, early drudgery of endless learning.

Student life developed into one sustained drinking bout. I recall on my first evening there being taken to a party by Count Nicolai Tolstoy, a friend of my family and myself who had been at Trinity for a couple of years. I became probably more drunk than I had ever been in my life. I remember bottles being passed round a circle of people, faces which were to become only too familiar to me over the next two years, a tremendous jovial atmosphere, and a paralysing sickness overtaking me in the middle of the night. This eroding process took place almost daily over the next six months as I 'acquired the taste' of Guinness.

I did not study and I had only seven lectures a week. These were supposed to be compulsory but frequently one's name was answered by one's friends. This was easily arranged.

I always recall one lecture which for some unaccountable reason I attended. It was a 9 o'clock morning lecture—as I think three of my lectures were—and I had missed most of them, but on this occasion I arrived from an all-night party determined for once to carry on the affairs of the day. There were four of us there out of a possible 32 but all 32 names were answered by those four people.

I can remember that the lecturer took it all in his stride, quietly ticked off the names and continued with the lecture. Then a Greek student came in about a quarter of an hour late. The lecturer looked at him with an astonished expression on his face and said: 'Is it yourself or your ghost that I'm seeing there at the door?'

They were great days really. There's no doubt about that. Had I not had that experience, I would not have travelled this course. If I had been successful academically I suppose that I would have foundered on or foundered in—both words are suitable—some legal career. So it was probably an excellent thing that I did lead the life of Harry while I was at Trinity.

I didn't eat very much, for I had very little money. We pooled our tiny resources to cover the cost of the coveted stout. I drank considerable quantities. I played billiards and snooker every day and became, at an amateur standard, relatively proficient. Again I was very competitive within a circle of friends. If we did attend a lecture we would immediately retire to the snooker rooms afterwards instead of going to the library to write up the lecture. It seemed more reasonable to progress through a few 'jars', then snooker, and probably a party at night.

At one stage, I became wrapped up in a poker school and gambled my life away—albeit somewhat cautiously I must confess. One pound or considerably less did not give me too much confidence in the success of my cards.

I had a friend who attended university at the same time as I did with whom I ran through four flats in a month. We used to leave these flats in the dead of night when the landlord or landlady wasn't around so we wouldn't have to pay the rent.

Then, two other friends, Michael Chamberlain and Chris Green, let me sleep on their sofa for two terms quite illegally. It was a most curious existence because I used to return to university for very demanding activities which were in no way concerned with its academic curriculum and recover during the vacation to prepare myself again for the tremendously testing abuse and assault upon my body—self-imposed.

I misused and abused my body to such an extent during those two years that for a while afterwards there were certain things I was unable to eat. In fact, since then, there have been many occasions when I have suffered from a somewhat troublesome stomach which may or may not stem from the excesses of that time.

I will always recall one particular instance. I was talking to one of my lecturers in Parliament Square in Trinity when a filling from one of my teeth fell out and rattled as it hit the cobbles. The lecturer stared at me and then remarked: 'Mr Barrington, I've always thought things were going badly for you, but you're positively disintegrating before my very eyes.'

I was known within the law school as 'the joker' because I never took my examination. Usually, I didn't appear at all and when I did actually sit an examination at the end of my first year I didn't spend more than ten minutes in the examination hall before tearing up my papers and stalking out—never to take another law examination. A pathetic performance really.

So I don't think I was looked upon too fondly by my tutor and other members of the legal science department.

In my second year, I travelled into the history school to speculate in the historical world and did complete an examination there—unsuccessfully. This was not surprising because I had probably not studied for more than three days and that under the influence of benzedrine just before I took the examination.

What with that and a succession of petty misdemeanours, the university authorities finally saw fit to ban me from the university premises.

I ended my career by throwing flour at a Nigerian friend of mine who was being 'commenced', getting his degree. I knew him very well and it was customary, although illegal, to throw flour on such occasions. Unfortunately, my aim was poor. My misdirected flour generously covered a very venerable Hungarian mathematician who was getting an honorary degree. Then came the rain; the flour solidified and I was forced to flee. The university porters were sent by the Junior Dean to apprehend me but I took sanctuary in the chapel in one of the pews and managed to evade their clutches. The university and I parted company—the fun had come to an end.

Since my success in the squash world I've regained contact with the university and, when playing in Dublin, have been received well, by my contemporaries. One or two of these, notably a well-known poet and a mathematician, seem to have found their way on to the academic and administrative staff of T.C.D.—further triumphs for Machiavellian minds.

In 1968 I was made an honorary knight of the Campanile, which is a sporting honour within the university, and my memories of Trinity College, Dublin, are tinged with particular affection. I reacted very strongly after leaving; I felt very wretched and miserable because I did thoroughly enjoy my two years there and made some marvellous friends. It always gives me great pleasure when I see them today, because when I left Trinity I was, I suppose, a candidate for the rubbish dump.

Now that fortune has favoured me, it is pleasant to meet them and to know that they are particularly pleased that my life has gone so well over the last seven years.

People say to me quite frequently: 'What about going back to university? Why don't you go back to do law? It's possible now and you'd get a better grant because, having achieved something, the education authorities would be only too pleased to support you because they know you'd be seriously involved.'

But, of course, I'm caught up in a sporting spider's web. This is my business; this is my career. I am a lucky man.

I played soccer for Trinity and because it was very much the Cinderella game it was particularly engaging to play. Frequently more than half the side would take the field under the influence of alcohol.

We had one glorious individual called Mike Harley who had quite a talent for sport. On one occasion, when we were playing quite an important match, we were awarded a penalty. We were all discussing who was going to take it when there was a cry of 'Leave it to me' and Mike Harley came charging through from the rear, planted the ball firmly in the back of the net, collapsed from a too recent and too potent measure of alcohol and had to be taken off the field. We won.

My old friend, Butch Stoddart from Birmingham, a Brummie with a broad Brummie accent, who looked physically the epitome of a Teddy-boy, but mentally couldn't have been more different, was a very capable footballer, but he reached such a stage of decomposition that he was unable to turn around on the football field. He just sort of leant backwards and fell over. We had a couple of schoolboy internationals but we all fell by the wayside really. There was a Nigerian, Eddie Wachuku, who had, in full, all the supple mobility of his people. His favourite trick was to try to dribble around all the opposing team, gradually winding up in more and more trouble before his final coup, a monumental shot at their goal from, preferably, our own half. It was quite a circus performance. Unfortunately there was no ring master so the performance remained entertaining perhaps, but totally uncontrolled. We had little success.

I played squash as well in my second year. Someone suggested that because my brother was quite good, I should be too, and the captain of squash persuaded me to play. The secretary, Paddy Heaney, arranged a game with the captain, John Gillam, just before the season in 1960. It was the beginning of October and for some extraordinary reason I managed to beat him. I hadn't played for over a year and I imagine he must have been totally unfit and out of practice.

But it got me into the squash team. I managed to retain my No. 2 position for all that season and had some great fun, although I was much better known for my ability to down an increasing number of pints every night. This was particularly evident when we went to Guinness's to play. We played Guinness's club, the Triflers, twice a season; it was always an away match and could hardly have been otherwise as they always put out an eight-gallon barrel for the two teams. So there would be six players and just one or two shrewd observers dealing with 64 pints of Export stout.

I was fascinated by football, still am, and I think it is the greatest game of the lot. Even though I'm totally committed to squash, I still have an ideal dream where I imagine myself as a player in a really big, successful league side, always slotting the goals of course.

I was an inside-forward or centre-forward, a crafty schemer with a useful left foot. They said that my right foot was for walking on but once or twice a season it produced 'the goods'; I played tennis for Trinity—for the first team in my second year and was coming through quite nicely again in that field too. I was beaten in the senior freshmen's final in that second year, after holding a lead of 5–2 in the final set. This greatly disturbed me and I threw a tremendous tantrum at the end. At least I was honest in those days and saw little point in hiding my fury when things went adversely. Now they tell me that I take my defeats well on the whole which doesn't mean I'm a good sport, but merely that I frequently qualify for an Academy Award on the grounds of a well-portrayed lie.

That was about the sum of my sporting activity, although one of my Trinity vacations did contain a brief and financially painful brush with the law: I received a £10 fine. It was really not the crime of the century because I only took a wheelbarrow. I didn't kill or cosh anybody, or even intend to retain the wheelbarrow. I merely took it when under the influence of alcohol one might in Earls Court Road, with one friend, who took another wheelbarrow, and another who, had he been successful, would probably have been arrainged with the crime of taking a steamroller.

We were not hanged for our crime. We were picked up by a squad car wheeling our wheelbarrows merrily down the Earls Court Road. We were taken to Kensington Police Station where we were charged with petty larceny, a fearful crime to which in court, rather naively, we pleaded guilty, having been rather conned into doing this by the police.

We came up at West London Magistrates' Court before Mr. E. R. Guest. Judge Jeffries himself could not have created a more disturbing atmosphere. He surpassed himself in the lucidity of his summing-up. He kept on talking about someone called Bruce, who had apparently lied. As neither of us was called Bruce, I fear the intricacies of the case were too much for him. My friend had stated that we were taking the wheelbarrows to Bruce's, whoever the hell he might have been. Had we been more aware of the law, we would have got off on that point alone.

But this was an expensive folly because I was fined £10, a great sum in those days. I had to go back into court to plead for time to pay. This was granted at the rate of £1 per week, but I was warned that if I slipped the country I would be sentenced to 28 days in prison. He really didn't need the powers of a high court judge and the use of the old black cap to scare the living daylights out of anyone.

I don't think my conviction is a stain on my character.

They've taken my glorious finger prints; they've found me guilty of petty larceny, a heinous crime. It was really quite pathetic. Quite honestly, there was a basic lack of a sense of humour. I didn't steal. Everybody knows I didn't. I was most aware of the fact that I didn't *need* a wheelbarrow. What would I have needed a wheelbarrow for anyway? But there I was, wheeling this particular wheelbarrow, which incidentally was not even recognised by the foreman of the wheelbarrow company. He said it wasn't easily identifiable because many wheelbarrows were similar. He was an Irishman so he had an instinctive feeling for me. He had to be virtually press-ganged into positive identification.

After all, they could have charged me with being drunk in charge of a wheelbarrow—driving a wheelbarrow under the influence of alcohol. This would have been an interesting skirmish with the law. I haven't followed my criminal career to any great extent although it must be confessed that while I was working at the Squash Rackets Association and times were still pretty hard, I resorted to cashing in the insurance stamp money as a short-term loan.

I will always remember during the course of this further folly receiving a letter from John Horry, the secretary, saying: 'Dear Jonah, I would just like to remind you that as far as we know there are no facilities for Squash Rackets in H.M. Prisons.'

This showed a very nice sense of humour I thought. And as far as my life of crime was concerned, that was that.

3

The Way into Squash—1963

Jonah Barrington

I was only nineteen and I seemed to have been left a legacy of nothing. I had no occupation; no qualifications, except reasonable 'A' levels which are not enough nowadays. I didn't know what I wanted to do. I had been somewhat cotton-woolled at Trinity by a university life so withdrawn from reality. It's a closed existence, very enjoyable at the time but so far removed from what goes on in the cut-throat adult world that when I was suddenly shunted out, it was a grievous shock.

I was unable to adjust myself for about four years. I drifted. I took part-time jobs. I taught in Spain; I had a groundsman's job; I worked as a coalman in Cornwall; I painted cottages in Devon; I went round cleaning carpets in London; my life seemed like one long hitch-hike. I didn't know what I was going to do. I think my father despaired of my future. He said that I should have been born into money because I obviously didn't belong to a generation of workers.

It was only in the autumn of 1963 that I began to pull myself round. I took a job for one term as a schoolmaster at a school near York. I then had some responsibility; I had a routine, I had to teach and become more methodical. I also used to coach the boys at football. This was very satisfying because I threw all my enthusiasm into it. The headmaster probably thought he'd taken on the York City coach. I looked upon myself virtually as the manager of the future England squad so the boys were drilled in all sorts of methods and ideas. Every available moment I had I put my team to practise. They hadn't won a match in years and they still struggled, but they certainly did better than for a long time. They enjoyed it very much more anyway.

It was at about this time that I began to have a considerable amount of trouble with my back. This condition grew continuously worse until it was diagnosed as a lumbar hernia. Apparently a small area of muscle at the bottom of my back had ruptured and turned septic. This was causing a lot of swelling and discomfort in the groin, because of pressure on a nerve, and only total inactivity brought any relief.

I was not then involved in any competitive sport and hadn't played any squash for about three years. After Christmas I went to another school in Buckinghamshire. More teaching, rugby coaching, getting myself more organised, gradually working out some pattern, getting my feet on the ground, perhaps growing up a little and setting myself up for the marvellous opportunities that I was going to have—even though I didn't know about it at the time.

My back operation in April 1964 was both another part of the process towards complete recovery and the turn of my graph, which had flattened out and was soon to start going upwards. I was recovering in Cornwall that summer from my operation when I first came into contact with the squash world through a player named John Mocatta, who had come down to Cornwall on holiday.

Since those rather successful days before I was thirteen, when I had collected nice cuttings about local tennis tournaments—the 'underhand wizard' serving the ball and all that—I had gradually fallen away: there were only a few more local cuttings marking my football career in the local side to show for this fallow period.

I'd always felt that I was going to be better at football than any other sport, but then a gradual and general deterioration set in until there was a nothing, a void where I really didn't do anything and where I seemed to be filled with a depressing emptiness. There seemed to be no hope and yet I was on the threshold of something fantastic.

It was extraordinary because, although I was only 23, I became a little desperate. I'm not interested in most things,

I'm interested in very specific things and the rest of it can go by the board. My nature isn't really very curious but what I'm interested in I'm really fascinated by.

But this was a very necessary stage I had to go through, because the reaction from it was tremendous application and a fanatical desire for success. One didn't appreciate the necessity of a measure of hardship, but this so often triggers off an appetite for achievement.

John Mocatta used to holiday in Bude, which is about eight miles from my home by the coastal road and about twelve by the inland route. There used to be a perpetual debate when my father was alive as to which road we would travel to Bude and tempers inevitably became frayed: we were an argumentative family.

John rang to ask my brother for a game. My brother didn't happen to be there on that day and my mother suggested that I should go along. I didn't have a squash racket and only agreed after considerable persuasion. John Mocatta took great pleasure in meting out punishment to a rabbit who grew more furious as he threw himself into it with great abandon if little skill. I hated being beaten. During the conversation afterwards he asked me what I was doing. When he heard that I had no job and was thinking of doing some more teaching, he said that there was a post available with the Squash Rackets Association, for a dogsbody and licker of stamps—what a compliment!

Anyway he contacted John Horry, the Secretary, and two weeks later I had a letter from him suggesting that I might come to London to discuss everything. This I did and I was offered the post. The S.R.A. was certainly no paradise on earth but beggars really can't be choosers. I took the job.

At the S.R.A. we were in a permanent state of cramp; I was very nervous, and I had lost a lot of the self-confidence that I had gained at university. I hated the job, which was indeed basically licking stamps, putting addresses on envelopes and reeling off reams of duplicating material. I did feel that John Horry thought I was some kind of cabbage. I may certainly have looked like one but I felt that I had a little more in my head than he thought.

My initial but abiding impression of that job was of being cooped up in a tiny room with this strange old gentleman who quite put the fear of God into me. It didn't help that (over the previous ten years), John had always had assistants who had become very useful squash players; and he made matters rather worse by commenting that I was the worst assistant both on the clerical and the playing side that he had ever employed. I would be told how his nominated teams of assistants would beat the England team although, of course, I would not be considered for this as I was then probably the worst club squash player in Britain.

I also recall that in the first month he put me in with a player from Durham called Ken Williamson. He was quite useful and exceedingly crafty but not up to the standard of players in London. He beat me and I can remember Horry looking at me with complete scorn when I had to explain that I had wasted two hours playing and having lunch, and confessed that I had been beaten.

One day I was feeling really miserable at the S.R.A. and thought: 'Well, I'll pack it in; I'll give in my notice and go home to Cornwall.'

I told Horry that I'd decided to leave. He shot up from his chair and said: 'What do you mean?' I replied that in Cornwall I could play at least more than I was playing in London, that I wasn't getting any coaching and there seemed little point in continuing.

Horry immediately got on the phone and started rustling up some games for me.

It was very good of him to go to so much trouble. He also tried to arrange some coaching for me with Nasrullah Khan who has played and still does play a very important part in my squash life. At that time, Naz had just left the Junior Carlton and was freelancing in London, particularly at Wanstead. One day he came into the S.R.A. office and John asked him whether he would coach me. Naz didn't know who I was or anything other than that he was staring at a peculiar long-haired individual, very long-haired by the standards of 1964, the early Beatle days. He was unable to coach me then because he didn't have the time and he was just about to take a post at the Lansdowne Club, where he could only play with members.

That was the second time that I had met Naz.

The first time was at the Junior Carlton Club in 1962. A friend of mine from university was playing there and had invited me to come along to watch. I have always had this feeling of wanting to play a role in the sporting world and as I watched this chap play I can remember thinking that I was so much better than ever he was at squash and that I really ought to make the effort. I thought: 'I'll go down to Cornwall, I'll go to the Bude court and I'll practise.'

I saw Naz, on that occasion, not knowing who he was except that he was obviously one of the famous Khans. I went up to him and said that I was very keen to play squash but that I had not played for a long time. I had a court near home. I was going to be there for some time and I asked him what I should do.

He said: 'You must bicycle to the squash court or if you can run, it is a very good thing. And when you get to the court, you must go on the court, and you must hit the ball 100 times up the forehand wall and then 100 times up the backhand wall. This is very good thing. And you must skip on the court. This is very good thing, very good practice. This will make you very good squash player.'

This was a very long time ago, almost three years before I actually came into the squash world. It was almost as if things were planned over a period of time, as if the gods weren't prepared at that stage to give me my main opportunity, but merely to bring me into contact with someone who—unknown to both of us—was going to be an important part of my life later on, and yet to withdraw me again for the time being. It was almost as if the fates were having a little joke, as if they were saying: 'In three years' time, we'll really put them together and see what happens, but at the moment we will just introduce them and let them operate quite separately still.'

So I was obviously thinking about making an effort even at that time. In fact, my university friends remind me that at university I used to say I was going to be world champion, which was not really extraordinary because it was almost always said when I was under the influence of alcohol. But they recall only too well that I would say: 'I will be the best at this' or 'the best at that'. It is obvious that this desire had been in my mind for a long time and it seems as if it was only a question of the time and the place. It just needed something to trigger it off and the difficulty I had with my back, the appalling void in my life during that period 1962–3, started the wheels turning.

At the S.R.A., for the first couple of months, I was of a very mediocre standard. I will always remember the depression I had because I was totally incapable of beating anybody—even if I could find somebody to play. I failed to get into the Hampstead Cricket Club team and once John Mocatta saw that I was not going to be as good as he had thought I might be, his interest naturally began to wane a little. I always remember being beaten 3–0 by a young university player, Chris Stahl, in the play-off for 5th place at the beginning of October, 1964. This was for the team which was going to play in the first division of the Cumberland Cup. It was the worst team in that league, but it was still first division squash and I couldn't make it. So initially people were fairly surprised when I appeared regularly at Hampstead Cricket Club after I had finished my work and played with somebody like Paul Millman, then only eighteen but now a leading player, and John Roy, a South African, who was in the team. A couple of times I played with Peter Richards, the Welsh international, but seemed quite unable to make any advance at all even if the signs of improvement were there—I was beginning to feel the rhythm of the game and my movement was becoming more natural the more I played. I had never led such a disciplined life: I was now slipping into the routine that I followed over the next five years.

It was less organised then; I had no thoughts on diet and, as regards eating, often slummed it. If I couldn't play, I'd go running. I remember running down to the barracks in Sloane Avenue, gaining entry by saying I was a member of the London–Irish Rugby Club. I'd just run until I felt ill. I thought that if I reached that stage, then it must be doing me good and that perhaps it would have some beneficial effect on my fitness. Progress through pain did seem to be one of the answers.

It was obvious that fitness was very necessary because whenever I played anybody I used to tire so quickly. I suppose my first breakthrough came after three months, when I beat Chris Stahl in a friendly game at Wimbledon. It was only a friendly but to me it was a tremendous breakthrough. The Cricket Club chose me for a couple of matches but when Pat Kirton, who was then an English international, beat me 3–0, I felt that it was like a man playing with a child. He didn't seem to be particularly interested in what was taking place and yet consistently advanced his tally.

He seemed to flit like a shadow around the court pushing the ball down the walls. I'd never encountered this sort of play and thought he was treating me rather contemptuously. In fact, I was doing him a great injustice because as I learned later, this was his natural game! He was particularly encouraging. Another time I was beaten by Mike Breckon who played for Wimbledon. He seemed to hit the ball very hard and I was unable to combat that type of game.

But after three months I started to gather myself together and gain a wee bit more contact. The S.R.A. had gone to Park Crescent with the other governing sports bodies under the C.C.P.R. organisation. We moved into offices there which were quite close to the White House and two or three squash courts.

So I joined the White House. I remember the fee of £5 was crushing financially. It was about half a week's wage. I used to go along there in the lunch hour to practise on my own. I would have half an hour, then get a couple of milk cartons

Jonah, aged 12, with his Kerry Blue 'Ricky'. This photograph was taken at their home in Cornwall by Jonah's sister Geraldine.

The English International team in 1966. (L to R, *standing*) John Ward, Tony Gathercole, Mike Corby; (*seated*) Jeremy Lyon and Richard Boddington. Jonah was frequently beaten by all these players early in his career, but he improved to such an extent that he captained the British team in the World Amateur Championships in the following year in Australia.

December 1966. Jonah had just won his first Open title, and Nasrullah Khan his second Veterans title. 'He had the same ambitions for me as I had for myself,' said Jonah of their master-pupil relationship.

Jonah and Mike Corby in January 1968 after Jonah had beaten his compatriot for the second time in winning his third successive Amateur title.

Geoff Hunt (Australia) 'There is no chink in his armour . . . unlike any other player he tires again and again and still comes back.'

December 1969. The Open Final. Exhausted but elated Jonah throws down his racket after gaining the winning point, with a dejected Geoff Hunt in the background. It was the end of a marathon game lasting almost $2\frac{1}{2}$ hours.

and sandwiches and go back to the office. That would be my first meal of the day because I never had any breakfast.

I always remember my first visit to the White House where each court had a coin meter. I put in two shillings and then practised for ten minutes before the lights went out. I was most upset at this and dashed upstairs to the receptionist. She said rather scornfully: 'Two shillings is for ten minutes. If you want a further ten minutes you must put another two shillings in and then another two shillings if you want to bring it up to half an hour.' She said this so contemptuously that I felt even more of a country boy than I did before. It was a difficult time. I was not interested in joining the social side of things after games because, quite simply, I couldn't afford to buy my opponent a drink. So I would avoid the bar and say after my game that I was going for a run.

If I did have a drink, it was just orange juice. I had a fetish about not taking liquid at that time. I would not drink any water. For about two years I never had a glass of water. I never had an orange squash. I just drank milk, orange juice, fruit juices. Now, of course, I put away gallons of water.

I was just moving blindly on because I had no specific ambition to sustain me. At the same time, my graph was slowly climbing upwards because I always improved on past performances against my opponents.

This provided great encouragement and continued right up to the Amateur Championship in January. I went through the qualifying round, not without a considerable struggle, and then managed to win my first round against an Australian Jim Moore, who was principally a tennis player, before losing in the second round to Sherif Afifi 3–0.

This angered me enormously and again revealed my tremendous competitive streak and clearly unsporting nature. I tried with tremendous enthusiasm against him but he made me twist and turn so many times, that three days afterwards my knees were still wobbly and sore because I had gone the wrong way too frequently.

Sherif was extremely good to me as he was one of the few people who would always play with me. He was very much better than me and was most helpful in practice games at Paddington. He also helped me in this match in the championships. He gave me a few points here and there and I think one game went to 9–7, but I was furious. I came off court and made a tremendous scene in the changing rooms. I can remember the Australians, including Geoff Hunt, were there. They must have been amazed. They had never seen me before, and certainly never seen a British player behave like that after a match. I was like somebody out of the Irish hills; but at least I was honest enough to show my real feelings!

But I was advancing and in February 1965, after I had been playing still less than six months, I made a further breakthrough in the East of England Championship by beating a previous holder, Ken Davidson, an established player in the North, and a South African, the eldest Woods brother, who was over here on tour. I came through to the semi-final before being beaten by John Ward, who was the rising star that year. He was improving all the time and very close to England standard. I think I actually managed to take a game off him in that particular match, but he proved to be the most difficult player of that season. Each time I played him over a period of two months I did worse than the last time, ending up with a county match at Bournemouth in March when he destroyed me for the loss of about six points. I can remember the tears flowing down my face afterwards and my brother being terribly upset and bothered about it.

It seemed that I had made all this effort and not shown much improvement.

That Easter, when I was detailed to run the West of England Tournament, I had my first encounter with Jonathan Smith, one of my predecessors as Assistant Secretary of the S.R.A., whom John Horry did admit in his more mellow moments was an even more incompetent assistant (on the administrative side) than I was.

Jonathan came from Yorkshire and played for England although, when I came into squash in 1964, he was out of the England team. He was sometimes known as Brother Jonathan because he taught at the Xavarian college in Brighton where the teaching staff consisted almost entirely of monks. He had entered this tournament from the South of France, where he frequently used to go for a few days of sunshine. On the Friday night there was no sign of him. His opponent got more and more fed up but, as I tried to placate him, a telegram was delivered 'Am arriving fast' signed J. N. H. Smith. It was about four o'clock in the morning when a telephone call from a call box came through from Jonathan Smith saying that he didn't know where he was. He had landed at Dover and had headed westwards. He wouldn't make his morning match the way he was going and what could I do about it? So I said I would delay and delay through the morning. Finally he arrived at about 2 o'clock in the afternoon, went on court and beat this bloke, who was a pretty good player, with no trouble at all.

Jon was very small in stature with a Herculean build, very stocky and muscular and very absent-minded; quite able to quote much of the works of Shakespeare verbatim but unable to remember where he put his socks. He always used to say as he appeared with one brown sock and one red sock: 'I've got another pair like this at home.' I used to play him at the Lansdowne Club and noticed one day he was looking particularly smart on the court. When we finished playing I had to play another bloke. I went to change my gear only to find that my lovely clean gear had been running round court with me on Jonathan Smith. He never brought any squash clothes with him to the Lansdowne but used to go to the drying room and open somebody's locker. He had one particular locker to which he returned time and again, plundering it of jock strap and all. This poor member of the Lansdowne Club would go away in the evening leaving his wet clothes in his locker in the drying room, where the temperature is 140°. Next day, he would be amazed to find his clothes sopping and everybody else's dry.

Jonathan once went from Brighton to play a game in London. He got on the train but at the last moment decided to hop off to buy a newspaper. Before he could get back, the train disappeared, carrying his kit towards Victoria, so Jonathan had to wait for the next train which was an hour later. Meanwhile, at Victoria, the baggage had come through. It was noticed by a porter, who thought that this baggage with a Brighton address should very rapidly be sent back to Brighton on the next train. Jonathan and his kit dramatically passed each other on the Brighton–London line.

Jonathan rapidly became one of my greatest friends, whether the wind blew fair or foul for me—he is not like the rest of the pack.

I reached the West of England final in April 1965 and was beaten by Sharif Khan in five games. On the way I beat Nigel Faulks who was graded above me. I was now becoming one of the best of the second group of players in Britain within six or seven months of starting to play the game seriously.

When everyone finished their season after Easter I decided not to take a break and every night after I finished work I went up to Hampstead Cricket Club to practise on my own or to play doubles with some of the club enthusiasts. This was a good variation, breaking the monotony, and quite often riotous fun. I did my running round the cricket field. I had no standard practice, and as yet I had not had the opportunity to be coached by Naz because I was still not a member of the Lansdowne. Nevertheless I struck so many balls during the summer that I obviously had to improve. Unlike the players who did something else in the summer, I had a second season in one year, so I was a much changed commodity the following October. I won the South of England Championship, beating Sharif Khan in the semi-final, after he had somewhat fortuitously let me off the hook, and then, in straight games, the dreaded John Ward, who had been a bogey of mine. This put me squarely in the limelight. In the next three months before the British Championships I was only beaten by Richard Boddington, Mike Corby,

Jeremy Lyon and Gerald Massy and I had a win over Corby which gained me a place as reserve, the No 4 position, against Australia in the Test Match.

I played Cam Nancarrow, who funnily enough turned out to be the player who gave me more trouble than anyone. He was more experienced and should have won but I played him rather better that I did on subsequent encounters. This was my first major breakthrough against a world-class player on a big occasion. I played a fairly safe game and he made mistakes. In fact, I was the only British winner. When I next played him eighteen months later, he was a different player. He had far more deception, hid the ball well with his body and knew much more about length.

It all stemmed from that summer period when enthusiasts like Nigel Faulks, Mike Hill, Paul Millman and myself would play and practise day after day. I was gradually becoming more specific although I had no proper schedule. I worked from day to day and did what I thought might be useful. I did a lot of skipping whereas now I do little or none at all. I didn't do any weight-training but I used to do press-ups and stomach exercises. My body was revelling in being really used. Whereas I abused it before, I was taxing it now in a different way, I was cleaning my body and preparing it for the assault which was going to take place over the next three years.

I worked at the S.R.A. until January 1966. I left after eighteen months, on the very day that I was beaten, 3–0, in the first round of the Amateur Championships by Richard Boddington.

I felt the time had come for a change. The S.R.A. had served its purpose by giving me the entré into the squash world. It was a job I detested; without a doubt it was the worst job I have ever had and because I disliked it so much, as always, being as I am, I failed to do justice to myself. There was no part that interested me that the Secretary was prepared to give me. If he had asked me to write on some of the tournaments or something like that I could have done a better job because this is something which appeals to me, but my mind could never become attuned to sticking on stamps, writing envelopes and reeling off reams of paper on the duplicating machine. This was, to me, systematic hell. I was relieved to leave the S.R.A. and so indeed was John Horry relieved to see me go. The babe he had taken on had grown too rapidly to monster proportions and was much too complicated a quantity. Mutual suspicion has remained.

Having been beaten in the championship, I remember not being in any way interested in taking part in the plate event and defaulted to Nigel Faulks in the first or second round. I badly wanted to watch the quarter-finals of the Amateur and as the plate matches were being played at the same time but at the International Sportsman's Club, I was not preared to wage war with Nigel for two hours while this really fascinating squash was going on at the Lansdowne Club. So, after winning the first game quite efficiently and losing the second, I walked off the court in the middle of the third. I wanted to get over to see people from whom I would learn something.

This was the one and only time I have retired in any match and I felt that I had a good enough reason, because the British players didn't appreciate the value of having these overseas boys in the championship and never admitted the possibility of learning from them. As they were here for only about six weeks, it was absolutely vital to make as much use of them as possible, to play with them, to watch them and to see why they were so much better than our own players.

In February, I became an Irish International. I asked my father, who at that time seemed to have made a remarkable recovery from his cancer of the larynx operation, whether he would prefer me to play for Ireland rather than England. This was what determined my choice and not, as has often been said, the fact that I had a chance to be Irish No 1 rather than British No 4. This was of no consequence as I had no intention of remaining English No 4 for very long.

My first international was against England and I lost in five to Lyon. Regrettably, I also lost in my second international to Ollie Balfour of Scotland before I beat Peter Stokes of Wales. I don't consider myself an Irish nationalist but I do count myself a Celt. I like to think that's where I got my fire and my pride from; my mother doesn't give a fig for anybody as she claims to be descended from the Kings of Wales. At international matches there was a special atmosphere of flowing informality which compared favourably with the establishment down at the R.A.C.—'No Ladies by request'. Always something rare and strange would happen in an Irish match and two members of the team, Barton Kilcoyne and Donald Pratt, have been particularly staunch friends, assisting me when I was financially hard pressed to the tune of £400. The President of the Association, Dick Tunney, not only provided me with accommodation but also an abiding memory of one international match. A totally committed enthusiast, he had dominated that famous day and seemed to have an increasing output of energy. The formal affairs completed, midnight long gone, Dick remained in command of a group still making merry in an inner sanctum of the Fitzwilliam Club. As even he began to feel the pace, so he took to a chair, like the rest of us I hasten to add. The pressure was now on but our worthy president still bravely resisted although an obvious slump was setting in: finally the chair and Dick parted and he lay peacefully recumbent underneath, quite unaware of the last minutes before close of play! It could never have happened in England—more's the pity!

4

Climax—1966

Jonah Barrington

Naz then set about me. I went to him at the Lansdowne Club and told him that I had come to a stage where I was one of the best players in Britain but that they were well behind the best players in the world. I said: 'I want to be a world-class player. I want to be a champion. What can I do? Will I ever do it?'

He said: 'We will see in three years.' He told my family this; he told Shafik; he told Jawaid. 'After three years we will know,' he said. But the old philosopher was wrong because in less than a year I had won both major titles; but in a more important sense he was right, because it had taken me three years to really organise myself, to become much more mature in my outlook and approach and to gain the necessary independence which must come with maturity.

In four years to February 1972 I have won three British Amateurs and five British Opens, the Australian, South African, Pakistan and U.A.R. Championships.

What Naz meant was 'we will see whether he will become one of the great players'—not just the best player in Britain. He had the same ambitions for me as I had for myself. I didn't know; I just had faith; I just hoped I could make it. But he believed that I would because I suppose he saw that I had uncontrollable enthusiasm and the necessary fanatical approach which meant I could apply myself all the time.

He started me off on a systematic schedule, the first I had ever had, giving me a methodical pattern of court training, talking to me for hours and hours, having a cup of tea and using the table as a squash court, talking tactics, talking players, talking philosophy, talking about life, pumping into me the need for constant self-discipline. He always said to me that if you are not disciplined off the court, you cannot be disciplined on the court—the two go together. No girl friends. He knew from his own experiences the emotional pressures which would come with this, particularly as I tended to be sensitive and highly strung. He turned away a girl friend because he felt my concentration and single-mindedness were beginning to waver. I could have killed him, but he was right at the time. There was a need for total involvement in squash alone and obvious sacrifices had to be made.

We had now established the master/pupil relationship, with Naz determined that he would not waste his unbounded knowledge, his talent for coaching and his enthusiasm, in scattering those seeds on stony ground. I would obey all his demands and all his dictates and he began to realise that I was the first person he had ever come across who was prepared to discipline himself to the degree he wanted.

I was prepared to go all the way because I badly wanted to succeed and I needed the help and encouragement of such a man. He had been a very famous squash player and was so highly respected that it was a compliment to me that he was so interested in my welfare and my future.

He made me practise; he made me train. He arranged a weight-training schedule for me which was paid for by two members of the Lansdowne Club, Bill Freedman and Roy Hart. He talked to me endlessly about the game, constantly reminding me of self-discipline, reminding me that everything must be routine, that I must be totally involved in this one pursuit if I was to succeed. To tolerate constant physical discomfort was merely the pathway to progress. I had more faith in this one man than all the rest put together. He was a fierce task-master but he loved me like a son. It was therefore a simple thing to obey his commands.

To carry out his schedule I had to take part-time employments. I took a milk round in the Earls Court area and had to get up at 4.45, a paralysingly early hour. I usually start the day pretty slowly and find physical effort particularly trying, but the milk round certainly provided me with a burst of fresh air at an early hour when the air was at its freshest. It also did a lot for my physical fitness because it was an outdoor job and I was on the move the whole time. Sometimes when I finished my round at about 11.00 a.m., I felt that I wanted to go to bed for about ten hours but, of course, this was the time to start training. I used to go to bed at about 9.00 at night and have seven hours sleep. I used to have an hour's sleep after my milk round from 11.15–12.15 and then go to the Lansdowne Club to put in some long bursts of activity before returning to my bed again in the early evening. I had no social life, no contact with girls. I became the *monk of the West End*.

I had this milk round until the end of April. I advanced even though I was on a hard training schedule. I broke through against Gerald Massy who, unfortunately, died in an air crash shortly after. I beat him twice, in the Cumberland Cup and the Lansdowne Trophy, both in the March of that season. I was obviously very close now to being the top player in Britain although I did not have the opportunity to play Jeremy Lyon or Richard Boddington again. So when the season ended in April, I still had to wait till later on in the year to see whether I could prove myself to be the British No 1.

When I finished my job as a milkman, I managed to get a job as a school teacher in Queensgate at a co-educational school principally for embassy children, many of them Japanese and Spanish. It was interesting, very entertaining and to some extent very exciting.

I fitted in my training as best I could. It amuses me to look back on the people who said that, of course, I was bound to succeed if I was not doing a proper job of work, but I did a proper job of work throughout the summer and at the same time went through all the frustrations of never being able to assess my standard because there were no matches. My only gauge was my matches with Azam Khan which began after Easter 1966.

I first went to play with Azam at the New Grampians Club,

which he owns. The tale of my first game with him is one I am fond of retelling in my clinics—of how I went along one day thinking I was pretty good and I saw this old joker with a bald head and ample waistline trotting around the court losing all the points to a member who wasn't particularly good. 'My God', I thought, 'if this is Azam Khan, he won't be of much benefit to me because I'm pretty well the best player in Britain. I suppose they weren't so good in their day.'

I booked a game with him and came to play. He met me very politely and took me on to the court. I condescendingly knocked-up with him and offered him the service. I didn't even spin the racket. We began to play and he beat me in approximately 18 minutes. I didn't even get one service, I didn't score, or at least I wouldn't have scored if Azam had not, when he got to 9–0, 9–0, 8–0, thought I was going to cry. He gave me a point, got the service back and beat me 9–1. I was totally unable to cry, I could not even make the effort. Physically and mentally I was shattered in less than 20 minutes and I was then supposed to be the fittest player in Britain. After only 20 minutes, this monstrous man aged between 40 and 50 had demolished me. This torture was repeated time after time throughout the summer, first twice a week, then three times a week, until by the end of the summer I was playing with him five or six times a week. If he was a little bit casual I seemed to get a little bit better; on other occasions he would really switch it on and I would be in terrible difficulties.

But it was an interesting summer because I had a job which I quite enjoyed and yet I managed to apply myself to this training schedule. I often did ask myself whether it was worth continuing and yet I knew that I had to if I wanted to make the grade.

When the school term ended in late July, I had to look for further employment. This was when I took a job as a dish-washer, as appalling a job as I ever had, because I started at 6.30 in the evening and ended at about 1.00 a.m.—one night I remember it was 2.00 a.m. I did this throughout that particularly warm August and September. It was really exhausting and, I suppose, part of the physical fitness build-up, but it was not of my choosing. It left me with very little energy for my training but I continued until my flat-mate, Dave Elliot, a Canadian, who was a lecturer in geology at London University, said categorically one night, when I collapsed from sheer tiredness on the stairs, that I was not going back to that job: he said he would finance me for the rest of my squash career if necessary rather than allow me to do that sort of work. Dave, Chris Kendall, Robin Waddell, Robert Johnson, Geoff Lemon—all shared a flat with me in Redcliffe Gardens and I will never have greater supporters. They lived the journey with me, fought all the battles and ministered to the wounds—and paid for my recovery!

I was then fortunate to find the easiest job I have ever had, from the point of view of conservation of energy. I became a model, a nude model for art students, privately and otherwise. I was terrified when I first posed in full view of forty art students, at least 70% of whom were girls. I forebore to put in my contact lenses because I felt that this at least gave me some form of defence. If I could not see them, in some strange way I thought perhaps they would not be able to see me.

There was quite a contrast between my rigid self-discipline and this sort of job and its environment. It was rather a strange contrast and quite typical of many situations I have been in during my life. It was much better because I was able to work in my own time, when I wanted to, and later on, when one or two people found out why I was doing it, they were very helpful and I made a considerable amount of money out of it. At the beginning I was paid about 30/- an hour, or something like that. By the end my money was doubled on private assignments, because, whether I was a good model or not, there was also a certain sympathy value.

It was an interesting year in that I did a variety of jobs all of which were helpful in terms of experience and went with the process of building myself up for the championships that were about to take place. I think it is essential to be involved to some extent in something else for a part of the day, away from the squash courts even though my thoughts more often than not will still funnel back to squash.

I lived my squash life at the Lansdowne Club where I have been surrounded by very close friends. These are not of the squash circle; they are not competitors; they are not my rivals; one's rivals are never one's real friends. These are people who have seen me rise from nothing to something and have lived and loved every minute of it. They helped me at the beginning when a free meal was a gift from heaven.

Arthur, his colleagues, the two Charlies and Ken, and Ron behind the old food counter, have been marvellous friends to me.

Whether I am up or down these people will cut the throat of anyone who decries me. Arthur Padget, of course, is an incredible character. He is a fixture at the Lansdowne. He is infuriating yet so lovable. He dominates; he is always firm; he tells me what I am doing wrong; he is an advisory service on all one's travels because he has been everywhere; he is the manual for all the byways of Britain, the restaurants of Britain and the quality of their food; he knows it all—and he does know it all—he is quite remarkable; he provided a therapy during periods of considerable frustration when I was very nervy, tripping uneasily along the high wire; he will always give one the relief of laughter. It's very comforting when one has a background like that. It's unusual and I'm grateful for it.

We had a puckish Irish barman, Jimmy Nolan, a keen sportsman, but who had spent too much time boozing and too little exercising. I decided it was time he turned over a new leaf and squash could provide the key. Jimmy practised and exercised every day—he could never have made a great player but he certainly became and looked one of the fittest specimens about. Jim is now the manager of a pub in the East End but still works out at the Mayfair Gym. The day 'Jimmy the Bar' faced 'Bill the Boss' on the Bruce Court was even recorded by *The Times* squash correspondent Rex Bellamy. Bill Marsden was the manager of the Lansdowne, fanatically involved with squash and a somewhat doubtful exponent of the game which he played with Naz at eleven every morning. My money was on Jimmy: I was refereeing—in the circumstances, useful—and Naz was the marker, but Jim's nerves were too much for him. Even the constant exhortations of the referee—Malcolm Allison had nothing on me—couldn't stave off defeat for him but, even worse, for my traditionally empty pocket.

I have always felt myself to be a man of the people. Outwardly I have all the Establishment qualifications, providing for 'satisfactory' social status, but at the same time I am much more at ease and happy with people from simple and humble backgrounds who are basically a darn sight more honest in their outlook than their public school contemporaries. I suppose I feel this because I come from the country where my great friends in my early childhood were Cornish boys and our varied enjoyments were very much country enjoyments—running around the fields, playing football, having bicycle races through the woods and across the streams. Before my brother and I went to school in Ireland, and when we came home from there or from Cheltenham for the holidays, we immediately fell happily into the company of these boys who were at the local grammar, primary or secondary modern schools. Certainly, while I was at Cheltenham, my friends were those I had left behind at home.

I played with Azam until the Open Championships. I was hit by the usual gigantic depression. Typically, I was going through a patch where I thought it was all hopeless and there was no point in competing. I can remember Azam demolishing me on three successive days by ridiculously easy scores and telling me afterwards 'You will be all right. You play in championships. You win championships. You win. You just play your game. You play your game.' And I did win.

I won because during the year I was remade, remodelled, refashioned by the Khans. They changed me; they made me grow up in that year. Years later, I had pressures and tensions that I found difficult to deal with but this was something else. I had grown up in squash in that year and I began to feel that I knew myself better. I was much more critical of myself and always so aware that there can never be any excuses. I found a method in that year and my life was made through the help I was given by Naz, with his boundless encouragement, and by Azam.

It pleases me to think that Naz and Azam derived immense pleasure from the way I came through and the success I had.

In the 1966 Open Championship, I was seeded No 5. As the old seedings were operating, I played the No 1 seed in the quarter final and No 4 played No 8. Now No 1 plays No 8 and No 4 plays No 5. Under the old system the No 1 seed had a more difficult time.

We knew that Taleb was suspect. Naz had always considered that Taleb would be open to certain methods of attack and was very confident that I could beat him. I did not know how considerable an advance I had made although I knew I had improved, when in October I beat Jeremy Lyon in the Strawson Memorial match for the loss of about three or four points. It was a demolition act, really, and when asked afterwards by the press what he thought, he said that I would have a very good chance of winning the Amateur.

Nobody else, of course, considered that Taleb could be beaten but we felt that there was some chance and I was continually boosted up on this theory by my coaches. I had a particularly hard four-game match with Mike Corby in the first round proper, the day before I played Taleb in the quarter-final. 'The best example of the British game,' Rex Bellamy wrote in *The Times*.

Taleb demolished Tony Gathercole, an English international, pretty efficiently so when I met him the following night I was very much aware of the fact that he was functioning fairly well.

He was definitely worried about me because he knew I was beating all the other players in his team in practice. He was obviously better than them but I had been doing it all with a track-suit on—after I had played Azam in the morning. I knew he was very fat because Fred Perry's shop told me that the shorts he wore were two inches larger round the waist than they had been the year before; so it was clear that our man had been idling in Cairo while I had been putting in this monumental effort. Azam said: 'He play winner, you return it. You win in the end.' Naz said: 'You must return the ball. When he plays a shot you must return the ball away from him and then see how many dead nicks he hits.'

He started trying to lose weight three days before the championships, by training in what looked like a boiler suit and thus revealing the first sign of weakness in his confidence. When we played, he refused to knock-up properly; he wouldn't even hit the ball to me. He hit a few trick shots, generally fooled around and provided the gallery with a laugh. He completely ignored me for most of the knock-up so it was obvious that he was very jittery and worried. He told the boys on reception at the Lansdowne how he was going to kill me off quickly, and when we started playing he went for a series of silly shots and paid the penalty for foolish extravagance. I won the first game and was well away in the second. Then, when I was leading about 7–2 he started his tricks, striking me with the ball, swinging wildly, knocking me over and using all his other terrorist tactics. I was still going quite well and felt quite strong until he really started pulling everything. He split his shorts; he cannoned into me; he continued to hit me with the ball—I think about 13 times in all by the end of the match.

But it was all to no avail. He did manage to win the third set 10–8 and he reached 5–5—in the fourth. It was a critical point but I managed to go away and, although I was very tired, hit one or two lucky shots to beat him.

The crowd went frantic and I was immediately the star of the show, no longer an outsider, and the new favourite for the title.

From *The Times*

Squash Rackets

BARRINGTON BEATS TALEB IN GRUELLING MATCH

Dazzling exhibition of technique

From our Squash Rackets correspondent

Jonah Barrington, a 25 year-old Cornish amateur who has sacrificed everything to squash rackets, had a glittering reward at the Lansdowne Club, London last night. He beat the Egyptian professional, Abou Taleb, champion for the past three years, by 9–4, 9–1, 8–10 9–5 in the quarter-final round of the open championship.

To say that is to imply that this was just a squash match. It was much more than that. It was a dazzling exhibition of technique and tactics within the framework of a brawl, in which Barrington had to take everything except punches. He finished with three bruises on the back and one on the jaw, three of them showing blood.

Asked for respite

Moreover, Taleb three times asked for a respite, twice to change his trousers, once to fetch a handkerchief. What with this, and the repeated occasions when Barrington was struck by shoulder, ball or racket, Barrington must have thought that Taleb was trying everything he knew to break the Cornishman's spirit and concentration.

It was the combination of all these factors that made Barrington's such a glorious triumph. First, he proved that he could beat Taleb at squash. Then he proved that his courage and concentration could withstand a multitude of distractions, not the least of them physical intimidation.

As in last season's final with Jawaid, Taleb's fine squash was marred by court manners that brought no credit to the professional game. This cast a cloud over what was basically a superb match, disputed at a furious pace—yet with Barrington time and again deceiving a man we had regarded as the crown prince of deceivers.

All Taleb's wizardry—notably his inimitable use of the reverse angle—came to nothing. Barrington read him like an open book and himself played masterful squash, mixing the long and short games with a cuteness and control that seldom faltered. The shot of the match was Barrington's—a winning volleyed drop shot from a shot of Taleb's that looked every inch an irretrievable length down Barrington's backhand.

The great thing was that in every way—courage, skill, and the ability to produce a winning shot when it mattered—Barrington was Taleb's master. The game as a whole, and the British game in particular, will be the better for it.

I was terribly inexperienced, having only been playing for two years, four months. I had still Amin to play and possibly Jawaid, but the pressure was now on me because I had knocked out the invincible Taleb.

Until that moment I had been an underdog—now I was placed in the rather unenviable position of being expected to win.

As it turned out, four days later, I was Open Champion, because I went on to beat Amin and Jawaid, the score 3–1 on each occasion, neither being at his best. Jawaid was not as fit as he might have been—I think he had a dose of 'flu at the beginning of the championships so I was lucky in that the circumstances favoured me.

I appeared much better than I really was. I had a willing heart and I was fiercely determined. I had everything to play for. I had limitless, bounding ambition. I was on a streak and nothing could stop it continuing, so things tended to run in my favour.

The Times

Open Squash

BARRINGTON IN FINAL

Jawaid through

From our Squash Rackets correspondent

For the first time in the history of the open squash rackets championship, two amateurs, Jonah Barrington (Britain) and Aftab Jawaid

(Pakistan) will dispute the final, to be played tomorrow evening at the Lansdowne and Royal Aero Clubs, London.

Jawaid, amateur champion for three successive years, was runner-up to Abou Taleb in last season's Open, and a year earlier was beaten by Ibrahim Amin in a semi-final. Since Barrington has now defeated Taleb and Amin in successive matches, the form makes encouraging reading for the Cornishman, though Jawaid has far more experience of the big occasion. They have never played each other before.

Record Takings

Barrington is the first British player to reach the finals since Michael Oddy did so in 1963, the year Taleb's reign began. The last Anglo-Pakistan final was in 1952, when Hashim Khan beat Roy Wilson. Tomorrow's winner will be only the second amateur to gain the title, the other being the great Amr Bey, champion from 1932–1937. To complete statistics,this year's takings are already certain to be a record.

Last night Barrington eclipsed the last of the Egyptians, Amin, 9–4, 4–9, 9–5, 9–3, and Jawaid beat his compatriot, Mohammed Yasin by 4–9, 9–6, 9–2, 2–9, 10–8. Yasin has never beaten Jawaid, though they have met five times in various championships. Last night the busy little professional had a match point at 8–6 in the fifth game, but put a backhand down after a total of 146 shots punctuated by three lets.

Barrington played a splendidly disciplined match against Amin, one of the finest artists to decorate the game. Conceding nearly nine years, Amin knew that to stand a chance he had to cut down the pace so that he could exploit his advantage in strokes and experience. He reduced his margin of error until it was perilously small. Barrington, equally, knew that speed and fitness would see him through if he could sap Amin's stamina—and blunt the edge of the Egyptian's game—by keeping him on the move and offering him little to hit.

Remorseless length

This, then, was the squash of the chess-board, a battle of wits in which bluff and deception played delightful roles. Moreover, it was disputed in the best possible spirit. Barrington began and finished at a hot pace, taking the ball early and thus keeping Amin under continual pressure. In between, Amin briefly gained control of the pace and took ten successive points—two in a row with backhand reverse angles that flickered and died like the last flames of a spent fire. Then he twice serviced out of court, and that was the beginning of the end.

The Times

FINAL

The champagne was flowing in Berkeley Square last night. British sport has another world-champion—a man fit enough to win a 53 minute final and then do press-ups in the dressing-room and plan Christmas training runs along the Cornish cliffs. It happened at the Lansdowne Club when Jonah Barrington became the first British player to win the Open Squash Rackets Championship since Jim Dear did so 28 years ago.

Barrington beat Aftab Jawaid, of Pakistan, runner-up last season, by 9–2, 6–9, 9–2, 9–2. To beat Abou Taleb (champion for the past three years), Ibrahim Amin (runner-up in 1964) and Jawaid in successive matches was an astonishing performance. Amin and Jawaid between them have won the amateur title five times, and Barrington has never before got beyond the second round in either of the big championships.

Now, 25 the left-handed Barrington did not take up the game seriously until 1964, but has since then devoted his life to it with almost fanatical dedication. Nasrullah Khan—the Lansdowne professional, who won the open veteran's title last night—has coached him. Azam Khan has sharpened him as a match player. Barrington himself has achieved and maintained a superb degree of fitness, and has matured fast as a tactician and match player.

All these labours last night bore the choicest of fruits, not least the fact that for most of its course the final seemed one-sided. Only in the second game, which Jawaid won from 1–4 down, was Barrington seduced into the hypnotic exchange of attritional driving to a length at which the canny Pakistani excels.

But in winning the second game, which lasted 20 minutes, Jawaid lost the match. He did not arrive in England until nine days ago and then, prostrated by a feverish cold, spent the worst part of four days in bed. He arrived at the final short of competition with only three matches behind him—though his semi-final had provided ample proof of fast-returning fitness and confidence.

Jawaid lasted almost twice as long then as he did last night. 'Jonah has improved so much,' said Jawaid afterwards. 'He is playing extremely well and is very fit. To play against him, an opponent must be really prepared. I got exhausted after the second game—and that is not me—so I played more shots. There was nothing else to do.'

'It was a hard and fair match,' said Barrington. 'I couldn't have wished for a more splendid atmosphere. Aftab and I get on well, both on the court and off it. My problem was working out why the second game drifted away when I'd had the lead—as it did against Corby and Amin. I was inveigled into playing his game—hard hitting to the back of the court—instead of varying it with chips, lobs and so on.'

From the start, Barrington made telling use of the lob, especially to Jawaid's backhand. In the match as a whole, Barrington hit 24 winners and 17 losers, Jawaid 7 winners and 20 losers (13 of them backhand). Barrington's strongest weapon was again his backhand drop-shot, though when Jawaid began to anticipate this the Cornishman had the sense to use his forehand drop more often, or turn his backhand drop across the court with a late flick of the wrist.

For the rest, Barrington used more shots, made greater use of the side walls and kept Jawaid quiet with some teasing 'clingers' when the occasion demanded. The Pakistani was made to cover too much of the court too quickly. Save for that second game, Barrington's tactical authority was never in question. It was a wonderfully mature performance by a man from whom maturity could not reasonably be expected at this relatively early stage in his career.

Barrington's exciting example has already put new fire into British Squash. In six eventful days he has turned the world game upside down, with the country of its birth once more at the top. A booming sport moved into a new era on the night the Celt beat the Pathan in Berkeley Square. As Bob Howe, that vastly experienced Australian sportsman, said afterwards: 'You've got a real competitor at last.'

The beating of Taleb was the platform from which I sprang towards winning the Open and Amateur Championships. Psychologically, it was a win which gave me a tremendous fillip, and the confidence to take on Amin and Jawaid in the semi-finals and final, feeling that I would not be beaten This confidence had evaporated slightly by the time the Amateur Championship came round about three weeks later, in January. We had Christmas and I had to suffer all the difficulties that arise after winning a major championship for the first time, under rather extraordinary circumstances. I felt that enormous cavern of anticlimax which seems to hit one afterwards. It's a depression whether one loses or wins because the build-up is so great that one way or another one still feels that tremendous let-down afterwards. I found it immensely difficult to build myself up mentally for the Amateur and to face two new dangers, the Australians Dick Carter and Ken Hiscoe, both of whom felt that perhaps my win in the Open had been lucky, although they obviously could not disregard it. This meant that they were going to be very much on their mettle and that they were determined to take the 'bloody pommie'. However, I was fortunate enough first to rediscover the right frame of mind to be able to struggle on against them and then win, albeit a little luckily. Hiscoe led me 2–0, 5–4 in the semi before he ran out of steam and Carter 2–1 and 7–4 before he made a rather strange error.

The Times

BARRINGTON'S CHANCE TO EMULATE AMR BEY

. . . Yet for two games Barrington was ominously tame and untidy. Loose shots were floating off the walls to offer Hiscoe inviting interceptions in mid court, and Barrington inevitably conceded a string of lets. Hiscoe, sharp and strong, pounced quickly and hit some glorious winners, notably with his inimitable cross-court backhand volley.

With Hiscoe in hand at 4–5 in the third game, Barrington was in deep trouble, 'I was back in the game,' said Hiscoe later, 'and I felt good. I was still playing well.' But Barrington was now hitting the ball instead of pushing it, and his game became correspondingly more accurate and positive. At last he was doing what he wanted to do—weakening Hiscoe's legs by mixing the long and short games at high speed.

Swept aside

It was a desperately tense crisis while it lasted (and that game took 24 minutes), a gruelling test of Barrington's quality as a competitor. He emerged with colours flying and the wind in his sails. Hiscoe led 3–0 in the fourth game, but soon he was getting stranded by yards. His backhand boasts have never been better, but his legs could no longer cope with Barrington's mixture of length and drop shots (the Cornishman made no kills).

For Hiscoe, the court grew bigger and bigger. In the fifth game, leaden-footed, he was swept aside in eight minutes by a string of merciless drops. The last of these produced an explosion of noise from the gallery: they had seen a Briton raise his game in adversity and fight back from the brink of defeat to run an Australian into the ground.

The Times

BARRINGTON FIRST BRITON TO WIN SQUASH DOUBLE

Astonishing recovery against Carter

by Rex Bellamy

The 27-day wonder is over. Jonah Barrington, a 25-year-old Cornishman who had never until recently gone farther than the second round of a big championship, last night completed the second leg of an astonishing double—the open and amateur squash rackets titles. The only other player to surmount this formidable twin obstacle was Amr Bey, of Egypt, in the thirties.

'Now I'm going to put myself through a pretty rigorous training routine,' said Barrington afterwards. He already works at the game for four hours a day. 'At the moment the gap between me and these fellows is marginal, I want to make it a gulf as big as the Grand Canyon.'

That comment shows what Barrington is made of: he will never be satisfied. But he was a lucky man to get off the hook at the Lansdowne and Royal Aero Clubs last night. For Dick Carter, of Sydney, led him by 2–1 and 7–4 in the fourth, only to put a backhand volley into the top of the tin as he tried to put the ball away to a length, having already drawn Barrington out of position.

That shot turned the match, because Carter did not get another point. Barrington won by 1–9, 9–6, 7–9, 9–7, 9–0. 'I didn't have the jitters,' said Barrington, 'because you can't afford the jitters when you are fighting for survival. Every point was virtually a match point. I played very tight squash and it put the pressure on him—instead of waiting for errors, he was going for winners. I thought "I've got to put him out now." When he put that backhand in the tin I was delighted to say the least.'

Barrington thought Carter played a 'foxy game', especially in varying the pace. For a good deal of the match the 27-year-old Australian was also much the more consistent, making notably good use of the side walls to draw Barrington to the front of the court.

What reduced Barrington to adversity was the defection of his tried and trusted ally, the drop shot, which time and again went not only into the tin, but also into the bottom of it. Because of this, his ability to pin Carter into the back corners was almost useless because Barrington had no reliable short winners with which to finish the rallies. He might have used the side walls for the purpose, but he did not.

Barrington was a game and 2–5 down before his game assumed positive shape. Even so, he had to work hard for that second game and lost the third, declining ominously after going well to reach 7–6. As Carter went to 7–4 in the fourth, it looked as though the emotional strain of the two championships (most amateurs regard the open event merely as a warm-up) had been too much for him.

Defeat was imminent. Barrington's brother and sister could no longer bear to watch. Goodness knows what was going through the minds of his club colleagues from Bude, who had come up to London to see the local boy make good. Then came that decisive back hander by Carter, one of the gamest and most popular players to cross the world to join us in London.

It was enough. Barrington, once again showing the resilience of the great competitor he is, swept through to two games all. So far the match had taken 93 minutes. But the fifth game, incredibly, was over in less than four minutes.

Barrington, still looking spritely, now had his man on a string. Carter was perhaps despondent after missing that chance in the fourth game. Certainly he was now weary. He tried to hit two winners. Both went down. At that, everything deserted him. His stamina had been broken and he could never get a rally going again.

With four winners of his own and five errors by Carter, Barrington romped through that last game in one hand, with only two lets to disturb the even tenor of his way. In ten minutes a great-hearted competitor had 'won' and lost his first major title—and the remarkable Barrington had made all of us proud to share the same passport. For the second time in 27 days, the champagne was flowing in Berkeley Square.

After I won the British Open and Amateur the S.R.A. decided to present me with a wooden plaque, which I suspected represented their opinion of my capacity for thinking. A dinner was laid on; people were invited; and typically, all the people who hadn't talked to me at all as I was climbing up the rungs of the ladder were going to appear and ask me to call them by their Christian names. We were all great pals now. I think I was allowed two special guests. Nasrullah Khan was one and Jonathan Smith was the other.

Jonathan was difficult to locate for not much had been heard of him for some time. Perhaps one could have got hold of him through Interpol or perhaps it would have needed some larger organisation, but in any event an invitation was sent out to him. Nothing was heard from him until, on the day of the dinner, at noon, a telegram arrived at the S.R.A. from Jonathan Smith which stated very clearly, very emphatically that he would be at the dinner that evening.

What puzzled John Horry, the Secretary of the Association, was that the telegram had been sent from Paddington some three miles away so God only knows what was in Jonathan's mind at the time. As Horry said mildly over the top of his glasses: 'He could have telephoned.'

Everybody arrived in immaculate suits—everybody that is except Jonathan. Jonathan was in agricultural tweeds with all the bottom buttons of his shirt undone, his underpants showing, one white sock and one brown sock and, dare I say it, almost a split in the seat of his trousers. But he and Naz were my most favoured guests for during 1965 and 1966, at times when the money that I was earning from my peculiar trades was not carrying me through as easily as I would have liked, Jonathan helped me considerably with financial aid as well as general encouragement. It is the people who help me when things are difficult who are the ones I remember.

5

Anticlimax—1967

Jonah Barrington

1966 was a great year for me but it was also the year in which my father died. He was dying for over six months of that year. He had first had some trouble with his throat in July/August 1964 just before I began to play squash seriously. When I came back from the South of France, where I had been on holiday, I found that every morning my father had a loss of voice, which later in the day would come back to its usual strength. He looked perfectly all right and he didn't feel any sort of pain.

I went away to work in London. About two months later, my brother rang up John Horry and told him what was happening: that my father had to have an operation to remove his larynx and that this was because of cancer—always I frightening word—I remember John Horry saying to me that a shouldn't be too optimistic about it. He said that this was an operation that could succeed but which at the same time depended on whether the cancer was dormant or whether it spread.

My father had his throat operation and this upset me terribly. I didn't see him until shortly before Christmas and of course he couldn't speak, although he was trying to learn to speak through a voice machine, which he held to his throat. He breathed through a hole in the throat and this obviously had a dreadful effect on him as talking was the spice of life to him. He was pretty depressed over that Christmas period and we were all relieved that he physically seemed to be in good condition although mentally it was as if he had just seen the last whisky bottle in the world destroyed—that would have appalled him too.

He seemed slowly to get a lot of his zest back. He talked

quite well in 1965 with the aid of this machine and he managed to get about a bit. He wasn't tripping around as freely but he was evidently getting his confidence back. The first news that I had of further trouble was in 1966 about a year and a half after the operation, which apparently is about the length of time it takes a cancer to regain its hold. I remember it because it was just prior to the General Election and father was chairman of the local Conservatives. I'd seen him again at Christmas 1965 when I was coming up through the squash ranks. He was very happy that I was doing this though in my own presence he said very little about it. When other people were around and I wasn't there he would boast about my exploits, but he didn't really know what I was doing. He nevertheless was patently thrilled that I was having some success in sport and he must have realised what it meant to me. He was also relieved that at last I had my teeth into something and had concentrated on it for two years even if he was still unconvinced that this was going to pay off financially.

He made a great effort to see that election out and then virtually retired to bed. He never went out again. He was given about six weeks to live. He had cancer everywhere. He was desperately ill and my mother told me that he was dying.

It was a dreadful shock. One rarely knows how much one loves somebody until he/she is taken away. He was going and I hadn't really spent much time with him for a couple of years, but the strange thing was that the more ill he became the stronger grew the rapport between us. He was very dignified. I don't think he suffered too much physical pain because the drugs were pretty effective, but mentally he must have been destroyed because, almost certainly, he knew that he was dying. At the same time, he tried to bolster up his own confidence by accepting the odd remark that I or someone else might make to the effect of how much better he looked today and how much stronger he was. Cancer comes and goes. The strength returned for ten days and went again and then, when all seemed lost, it returned again. It's weird; it's as if there's something eating a meal, as if it satisfies its appetite and goes away to sleep for a while and, having slept, becomes hungry again and needs another meal. This slow process of dreadful destruction lasted over six months.

That summer, when I was teaching at the school in Queensgate, I went home every second weekend and at one stage three weekends in a row. Having been told that my father was dying and that he only had so long to live, I wanted to get down whenever possible. I was up and down like a yoyo always wondering when I said goodbye to him whether I'd see him the following weekend. Looking back, I don't know how the devil I managed to end the year successfully. I doubled up all my training schedules, did an enormous amount of work and at the same time had this mental pressure behind me.

My mother was absolutely fantastic. She never seemed to waver at all. My father never complained; he just grew weaker. In October my defeat of Jeremy Lyon was a tremendous start to the season but by this time the old man was not really capable of focussing his mind on exactly what I was doing and how much I had achieved. His concentration went; his power to concentrate on even a book was almost non-existent. This was very sad because reading had always been a special joy to him. In whatever way he might have sinned, if one looks at it that way, he was certainly being paid back most horribly.

I went with a team from Cornwall to play in Dublin for a week. I was violently ill from some filthy disease in the stomach, strangely after visiting Guinness's, my old battle ground, where I was supplied with milk. This, of course, was regarded by my old friends there as a due punishment for having taken the pledge. I then had to go to Manchester to play in the North *v* South match where I managed to con my way through my match against Clive Francis despite having thrown up on the plane coming over and again when I was in Manchester.

On the night I returned to London at about 11.30 there was a message that the old man had died that evening. I went down to Cornwall on the Saturday morning for the funeral. About nine weeks later I had the two major championships of the world under my belt. He missed that and so never saw me fulfil myself at all; but when he died I think he felt that at least I was on a steady track and wasn't straying all over the place; that I did have some purpose in mind although he wasn't altogether sure what it was. It was a shame that he wasn't able to see any of my really big wins, or even to read about them, because he loved that even in the early days when we were playing local football.

My self-confidence was snapped by Trinity and the aftermath left me with a feeling that I had dismally failed and that I had no ability toconcentrate on anything for any length of time. I wanted to achieve something but too readily I was prepared merely to daydream it. I had a terrible feeling that I was basically too weak, mentally and physically to be successful at anything.

This drove me on. I really wanted to show those who had knocked me, who had observed that I had fallen by the wayside, that I was going to rise above all of them, to make myself a reputation that would be the byword for discipline and the complete athletic existence. This was almost inherent in me but I needed to purge myself of a lot of other things first.

The severity of my life bothered my father slightly and indeed he always said that I did things to extremes. When I go out to train I always hurt myself, though some days this period will be shorter than others. I will never go out and run within myself, or do any exercise within myself for a whole session.

That year hardened me to a tremendous degree. My father's death that November still came as a really savage shock. When I think of it now I wonder how the hell I managed to concentrate so well on the championships. Other people would have said; 'Oh well, that only shows that the death of your father didn't mean as much as you are saying now.' But I remember very well that it upset me far more than I thought it would. Because I knew he was going to die, I felt that I would not feel the blow when it fell because I had been preparing for it. But when it happened it was like having a limb cut off: it's gone away; it can never be transplanted; it can never be replaced. He's gone and because we'd talked so much, there was, in the end, no friction. It had been broken down until there was only love and understanding.

That year was a traumatic year without any shadow of doubt and it is amazing that I managed to win those titles with only a reasonably efficient technique and a rather flimsy foundation of fitness: but it was, nevertheless, a tremendous improvement on what I had before. My greatest asset was probably that I came from nowhere and the other players weren't really prepared for me. Once they'd seen me and I'd managed to get away with those two competitions all the players, particularly the Australians, thought: 'Right. Bigger effort needed.'

The British and Australian Opens became just as hard to win as those two first championships—and without that incredible pleasure of beating someone you'd never beaten before and making the breakthrough. Since 1966 there has never been a breakthrough in this way and the satisfaction has also never been quite the same.

The anticlimax, the depression within me, was absolutely enormous because the two major world titles at that time were the British Open and the British Amateur. Suddenly, having been a nothing and a nobody in squash, I had won the two most important championships. This had not been done since 1938 and then by Amr Bey, the legendary man from the U.A.R., so where was I to go from there? I had only been playing the game seriously for two years five months. As far as winning squash championships was concerned I had won the major titles, so anything that I did after this would be less of a triumph, or so it seemed.

Now, several years later, one can appreciate that this was not so at all. There were so many more pinnacles to be climbed and it is clear that I am not going to succeed every time. I have had to fight my way back on a couple of occasions. There will be many such.

The first official World Amateur Championships were to take place in August and September that year, in Australia—the team championships in Sydney and then the individual title in Melbourne. The individual title was called the International title but, of course, was really the first official World Amateur Championship.

For this I was seeded No 1, but I was still inexperienced. In Australia I was going to play with a ball which was foreign to me. I could not appreciate the difference between our ball and theirs. Hiscoe and Carter had muttered a few vows and oaths about what they would do to me when I got to Australia and how difficult I would find adapting to the Australian ball and conditions. This was most certainly borne out when I arrived in Australia in July that year. The furthest I had ever travelled overseas was to the continent. I had never had a time-cycle change. They didn't come any greener.

I was full of nervous energy. I trained very hard on arrival instead of going to bed and just eating, sleeping and walking for the first four days to adapt myself to this enormous change in time.

I didn't recover from this maniacal work-rate for probably three weeks. A doctor later told me that I could have done myself a considerable amount of harm through the amount of activity and the energy I expended on arrival. I had practised with the Australia ball in Britain for three or four months prior to going out there and was still beating the other British players quite easily, so I felt that I must have improved and that Hiscoe and Carter had better watch out.

I felt fairly confident that I would be able to stand on my own and make a really good showing. This premature confidence was soon dispelled because within ten days of being in Australia I was obliged to play two matches for the British team against New South Wales and another selected side. In one I played Nancarrow and was beaten 3–0 in 18 minutes and in the other I played Hiscoe and was beaten 3–0 in 19 minutes. In neither match did I really get up a sweat for the single reason that I was always buried behind my opponents and the rallies were short, because they hit so many winners. I was completely confused and ill-equipped to solve the problem.

The dilemma was simple—how the hell was I going to win? I also had difficulties within my own team. These difficulties accummulated over the next six weeks and this too was a bit of a burden. Basically I was so puzzled, so bothered, and so upset by what was happening to me that I couldn't see what I could do about it.

It was only through some very kind treatment from a man called Aub Amos when the side went up to Queensland to play in the Queensland Championships that I managed to bring myself round to produce a semblance of form.

I did win the Queensland Championship, playing reasonably well by the end of the week. Nobody would have given me a chance at the beginning, because I had completely lost confidence and could not hit two balls in the same direction. I was really frightened. I wanted to bury my head in the sand, to get away. I could recall Jawaid saying to me once, that on his first trip to Australia all he had wanted to do was to get on the first plane home because things were going so badly. He was being chopped so easily, his pride was taking such a hammering that he just wanted 'out'. The Australians have a talent for rubbing salt into the wounds.

One incident which illustrated this involved Dawie Botha, then South African Champion and No 1 player. It did have a funny side although it inflicted such a psychological blow that Dawie has never quite recovered.

The South African team was in Melbourne playing a warm-up match against New South Wales at Albert Park, which is virtually where Geoff Hunt was brought up and where the name of Hunt features very prominently on all the honours boards. As Dawie says 'It's 'Unt's court. If it's not Geoff 'Unt it's Bill 'Unt, and if it's not Bill 'Unt it's Old Man 'Unt.'

On this occasion Geoff was at his fiercest and won the first set 9–0. Dawie was just towelling off, vaguely wondering what to do when down the steps rushed Bill and Vic Hunt to grab hold of Geoff and give him a tremendous pep-talk.

'Man, what are they telling him?' said Dawie. 'What are they telling him?' he demanded of his advisor.

When Geoff won the second game 9–0 exactly the same thing happened. Down the steps flew Bill and Vic, talking, talking to Geoff as if he was struggling for his life.

By now Dawie was pretty distraught. 'What *are* they telling him?' he said. 'What *can* they be telling him? He's done nothing wrong yet.'

After Geoff had also won the third game 9–0, Dawie still couldn't work it out. Days afterwards he was still asking 'What were they telling him? What were they telling him?'

But I did gain a little bit more confidence through my win in Queensland. I only beat Mike Corby, but he and others had been beating me in practice. Peter Stokes only got four points off me in the semi-finals and Corby, after winning the first, won only four more points.

So at least I had put myself on top of my own players, which was a start. When I went back to Sydney I had about five or six days before the team series began. I played well in this series; I found that I knew now what I had to do. I had to volley more, to go forward. I was better than the players at No 1 in most sides so I was able to concentrate on doing this. I was quite effective and won all my matches 3–0. It would have been a clear slate had I managed to slot Hiscoe when we played Australia.

I had a two sets to love lead and was leading in the third but he fought his way out of it. I was a little overconfident at that stage, mainly because I was so happy to find myself in the match and moreover to have him in some difficulty. He got home 9–5, in the fifth. It was a very close match and there were some appreciative comments made after it.

Uncharacteristically, I didn't feel bitterly disappointed about losing. I was relieved because at last I had gained a measure of self-respect. I had reached the frame of mind where I was happy to have just shown something. But this was not the real Jonah Barrington.

We went down to Melbourne where I played reasonably well and then was beaten by Nancarrow, who then became my bogey man until I beat him in February 1969 in the semi-final of the World Amateur Championship.

The Times

BARRINGTON BEATEN IN STRAIGHT GAMES

From our Special Correspondent—Melbourne August 24

The British challenge for the International Squash Rackets Individual Championship ended in the semi-final round here this evening when Jonah Barrington lost rather sadly and certainly unexpectedly to Cam Nancarrow, of Australia, in three straight games, Nancarrow won by 9–7, 9–6, 9–7.

Barrington's chances of reaching the final were thought to have been improved by Nancarrow's defeat of Dick Carter in the previous round. Two years ago Barrington and Nancarrow had played each other in London as reserves in the match between Australia and Britain when Barrington emerged a clear winner. Although both players have progressed since then, it was thought that Barrington had shown great improvement.

Below his best

Nancarrow played the more aggressive game and deserved his win. Barrington played almost entirely on the defensive, hitting the ball only half as hard as his opponent and made many more mistakes than usual.

His supporters waited expectantly for the real Jonah to emerge, but except for an occasional shot he played well below his best.

Nancarrow led 6–2 in each of the first two games, and if Barrington's play is to be praised it is for the way he fought back. The lead of 6–2 in the first game was whittled down to 7–6 before Nancarrow won it at 9–7, and in the second game Barrington scored three points after his opponent had led 8–3. In the third game Barrington, for the first time, got in front to lead 5–3, but weak strokes gave away the advantage and Nancarrow reached his first match point at 8–5 when Barrington snatched at a volley pulling it in on to the tin. Barrington courageously saved five match points, but at 8–7 he fell in going for an almost impossible 'get' and conceded victory.

I was always struggling. I have always found Nancarrow very difficult to play and he dealt with me quite easily. This was a dreadful humiliation. I kept people about me as long as I could but I finally had to go to bed at about 2.30 a.m. Being on your own is the worst feeling in the world. I had hours of misery and self-pity, but all I wanted to do was to come back to Australia to see if I could win their championship. I played out that tour with the burden that I had failed. I failed in Australia because I was No 1 seed and did not justify it. I went on playing for quite a time afterwards in New Zealand for the British team, playing some good matches, some bad ones, and getting more and more tired because the travelling was pretty arduous and the hospitality so lavish.

I felt that the other players, certainly Corby and David Brazier, placed an extra load on me. Brazier's approach to the tour seemed diametrically opposed to my own. We were sent there to do a job of work. We were under an obligation.

A lot of money was raised to send us there, and whereas we intended to enjoy ourselves at some time, there was a clear priority to try to win the World Championships. David could not have given more of himself on court but that by itself is too often insufficient without the same attitude to preparation.

Corby seemed reluctant to play second fiddle to anybody and did himself a powerful disservice by not preparing and not allowing himself to be prepared mentally for specific matches. So much so that his record in that series was diabolical. His 3–0 defeat in the last match against Trevor Johnston of New Zealand was a particular anticlimax to the series and very nearly took us back to fourth position, which would have been disastrous, even compared to the very poor second to Australia which we achieved.

Peter Stokes, as always, did his best. He is not the world's greatest match player. He finds it difficult to produce his best squash on the big occasion. This is not his fault; it just happens to be so. He was certainly the most efficient player in the side, including myself, and was always most responsible and mature in his outlook. To play for Great Britain is the supreme domestic honour and I cannot understand players who are not aware of this. Sometimes I have felt that many of those chosen for this country are more concerned with the wearing of the tie and blazer rather than a full expression of themselves within the playing of the game. A social awareness and sartorial elegance are commendable but surely well down the field in the list of priorities. Teams are sent overseas with a task to fulfil and nothing must make that essential of subordinate interest.

Corby was suspended afterwards, not because of this tour in Australia, but because he left the team in New Zealand without permission. To leave at the halfway stage, as he did, was unforgivable although in retrospect there was a funny side to it.

We were in Wellington with Mike greatly looking forward to a battle with the New Zealand No 1 Trevor Johnston, who had beaten him 3–0 in the world championship series. Mike refuted the suggestion that Trevor was a better player and when the opportunity came to play him again I agreed that he could play No 1 and I would play No 2 against Palmerston North. We went to bed that night knowing that we were going to be picked up at about eleven by some people from Palmerston North.

We were not going to have to get out of bed before half past nine, which was bliss because we were all short of sleep. I was sharing a room with Mike; Paul Millman, who had joined the team because David Brazier had decided in advance not to tour New Zealand, was in with Peter Stokes. Both Mike and I were tired and went out like lights—or I presumed we did. I certainly did, but was woken at some unearthly hour by someone crashing round the room. All sorts of things were being thrown about: cases here, ties there and clothes up in the air. I looked at my watch. It was about 8 o'clock. It was Mike or as I affectionately call him sometimes, Tricky Micky, thrashing backwards and forwards throwing things into cases.

'For Christ's sake, Tricky, what are you doing? We aren't being picked up until eleven. This is the only time we've had to get a sleep and you're buggering around.'

'Oh well, my girl friend's going to the West Indies and it's the last chance I'll have to ask her to marry me. I've bought her a ring and I must go. It's my last chance and my plane leaves in an hour.'

'What about the tour? We've got another five matches to go, what about that?'

'Oh you'll be all right. Paul Millman: he's with us. He'll be all right. A good lad, Paul. He's playing very well and anyway you can play twice, can't you?'

I mused on that for about five seconds and accepted that he was going. He was bent on departure and I was fed up with trying to keep him interested. I was still suffering from my demise in Melbourne so he could get the hell out of it. As he headed out of the door carrying one of his bags, Peter Stokes suddenly appeared in the doorway with astonishment in his face.

'What on earth are you doing?'

'I'm going, I've got to catch a plane, etc etc etc.'

'But you can't. We've got a tour to complete.'

'I'm not completing the tour,' Mike mumbled and off he went down the stairs.

Peter came in as I lay there and said, 'What are you going to do about it?' I appraised the situation judicially and delivered my verdict: 'Nothing,' I said.

So Tricky Micky left and the three mangy lions were left to complete their tour of New Zealand. Mike said to the newspapers when he got back, and after he had been suspended, that he had

had to leave early because he'd never been told how long the tour was. This and many other extraordinary statements bore no relation to the fact that he had pulled out on the pretext that he was rushing off to the West Indies to propose marriage to his girl friend.

The tale is, of course, well known that when the other players, Peter and Paul, reached Mexico City, up popped Tricky Micky. He had, in fact, arranged to meet David Brazier and then go on a tour of the islands, Los Angeles and Mexico City. He didn't want to miss out on what 'La Bra' was going to do; but Mike did have the embarrassment of meeting on the very plane in which they left Auckland the last fellow passenger in the world that he would have wanted to see: the Secretary of the British Squash Rackets Association, John Horry, who, just by chance, had come through from Melbourne to Auckland en route for some other distant part.

'Good God, Michael, I thought you were in Palmerston North. What are you doing here?'

Tricky muttered something, hastened off round the corner and boarded the plane. Tricky was at one end of the plane, Horry was at the other and David Brazier was the liaison officer.

Paul Millman later related to me in a letter that, having reached Mexico City, Tricky appeared and said: 'What about this tour of the West Indies we are all doing?'

Peter Stokes, who had taken on himself the awesome burden of captaining Paul Millman, replied to Tricky's query 'Where are we playing?' with the words 'You're not playing anywhere; you're not in this team.'

'I am in the British team,' said Tricky.

'No you're not,' said Peter. 'You're not in it; you left the British team; you're not in it; I'm the captain and I say you're not in it.'

When they boarded the plane for the West Indies, Tricky again was at one end of the plane with Peter at the other and Paulus Millmanus, now the liaison officer, beset by Peter Stokes saying 'He won't be in my team', and Tricky desperately trying to re-establish his credentials so that he could avail himself of the undoubted hospitality which was to flow in the West Indies.

When the plane landed, two players in British blazers could be seen sprinting across the tarmac, with Stokes as soon as he spied somebody who could have been part of the reception committee pointing out Mike Corby and saying: 'That man is not in my team'—to the amazement of their hosts. So poor Tricky was, in fact, banished from the fold. He was last seen on that particular tour, as Paul and Peter were driven into town, about half a mile from the airport trying to thumb a lift.

When Mike returned to Britain he was reported. The S.R.A. felt that he should have completed the tour of New Zealand because the New Zealanders had laid on the tour at some considerable cost and put forth their hospitality. For an international player to opt out for some nebulous reason was unsatisfactory and therefore he was suspended for three months. He was punished but, most unfortunate of all, he was unable to recognise what he had done. For all that, the remarkable quirks of his unpredictable nature contribute a liveliness to the squash scene which would be sadly missed—by me anyway.

6

Targets—1968

Jonah Barrington

When I left New Zealand, I went back to Australia. I didn't know what I was going to do and I certainly was very unsure about my future. I remember arriving from New Zealand at Sydney Airport, getting a paper and seeing a photograph of myself with the headline 'New Australian Jonah Barrington'. This upset me intensely and made me very determined to leave Australia as soon as I possibly could. There was a story that I was joing to join a racket firm called Sunflex who had been interested in my using their equipment. Somehow the story had been leaked that I was going to remain in Australia but I had no real intention of doing so.

In fact, I played some exhibitions in Australia ending up in Perth. I played in a tournament there and actually beat Cam Nancarrow in the final in five games. I then took a flight to South Africa.

I had been in communication with South Africa and the South African officials had suggested that perhaps I should return that way. The first week in October, I arrived in Johannesburg for my first visit to South Africa and spent about three-and-a-half weeks travelling and playing in South Africa and Rhodesia before returning to Britain. I played in exhibition matches and gave the first of my coaching clinics.

When I was told, shortly after landing in Johannesburg, that they would like me to give a coaching clinic, I was aghast. I said: 'Well, how do you mean, give a coaching clinic? I am an amateur anyway. I can play if you like. . . .'

'Well,' they said, 'we have heard that you are a great talker on the game. We would like you to give a clinic. It will be at the Wanderers Club.' This is the main court in South Africa and holds about 350 people. There weren't 350 people for my clinic; there were only about 50. But it was bad enough.

There were players and officials from the South African Association there and I had no idea what I was going to talk about. So in an hour of hasty thought, I worked out an idea, a skeleton plan for a clinic, just praying that the words would come when I was on the court. I think this was the first occasion when I suddenly realised that I could talk to a gallery full of people. Even though there wasn't a background of confidence I was still able to talk, and as I became more sure of myself during the course of that first clinic, so I began to speak more confidently about my sport. Basically I related what I had been taught by Naz and told a tale or two about him as I went along.

I remember watching the faces as I talked and feared for the worst as a collection of stony faces returned my uneasy glance. At the end, however, I was told that they were enormously pleased with it, that everybody had thoroughly enjoyed the clinic and everyone was rather surprised that I was able to talk about the game so articulately. This was my first clue to what I might be able to do as a professional because during that stay in South Africa I went on to give a number of clinics and talks in Johannesburg, Cape Town and Port Elizabeth. It was a great foundation for my career as a professional.

It made me even more determined to change my status. I had decided to do this if I had won in Australia in 1967, but this was deferred because I wanted to have another crack at winning the World Amateur title. So I had to live by hook or by crook for another 18 months, and this gave me a valuable breathing-space to plan the future.

I was definitely going back to Australia. I resented the way I was treated in Australia, not by the best players but by the great Australian squash public, who devoted a considerable amount of time to talking me out of the game before I ever went on to the court, and who relished rubbing salt into the wounds after I had been beaten.

Back in Britain in November 1967 I worked out a campaign of activity for the next 18 months.

I set myself certain targets along the way but without worrying too much whether I reached them all. This point must be made because in one or two of the papers I seemed to be a bit of a Cassius Clay, which is no bad thing if you have got Cassius Clay's ability—which I don't have.

Evening News

JONAH BARRINGTON

Here's a British Sportsman who says,
'When I lose it's like a knife-wound'

by John Oakley

Jonah Barrington, Britain's most dedicated sportsman, has set himself a herculean 15-month task to prove he is the world's finest squash rackets player.

Barrington, whose training schedule would make England's top soccer stars gasp with amazement, means to win seven major championships running—a feat that most people feel is absolutely impossible.

Says the irrepressible Jonah: 'First, I want to win the British Open next month and then the Amateur title in January.

'Then the championships of Egypt, South Africa and Australia followed by the British Open again next year.

Target

'Finally I want to round it off by winning the World championships in this country in February 1969.

'If I can do all this, then I will turn professional knowing that no one can dispute my position as the world number one.'

Jonah is no cocksure Big Head. He believes it can be done.

Though he became the first British player to win the Open and Amateur titles at the same time last winter, he is a disappointed man.

'I won almost everything going in the last 12 months,' he says, 'but I lost in the semi-finals of the world championships in Australia.

'That was the big one and if you don't win it you can't call yourself the top man.'

Australian Cam Nancarrow was the player who spoiled Jonah's year in the world championships but since then the British star has proved his superiority over his rival.

So he looks forward to the coming months with confidence and no excuses in the background.

'I can't stand players in any sport who, when they reach a high standard, are not dedicated. The type who say when they get to 40, "If I had trained a bit harder I would have been the champion".'

Password

'When I get to 40 I want to say "I was the champion".'

Dedication, in fact, is Jonah's password. He took odd jobs such as part-time modelling and a milk round early in his career to leave as much time as possible for squash.

'When I lose,' he says, 'it's like a knife wound in the stomach. I hate losing.'

He trains in Commando fashion, plays four hours a day and never loses his zest.

He means to be 'the Greatest' and with his un-British attitude—'Dash it chaps, it's only a game' is not in his repertoire—he is likely to reach his goal.

I considered my targets as incentives for work and training to the final goal of the World Amateur title in London in February 1969.

So I had the British Open in December 1967, the Amateur in January 1968, the Egyptian Open in March, the South African Championships in July and in late August the Australian Championships in Perth; the last was obviously my chief goal for 1968, as it was virtually the World Amateur title of 1968.

This would be followed by the British Amateur in December, the Open in January 1969, then the Team series, and finally the World Amateur title in February. There were eight titles. I started to knock them off one by one.

1968 was my best year so far because I took the British Open without losing a set. I dropped one set in the British Amateur final playing with an unfortunate shoulder injury which necessitated pain-killing injections from the quarter-final stage onwards.

I had a clean sheet in winning the Egyptian Championships beating Shafik and Taleb; I came back to Britain and continued my schedule in Cornwall, went to Kenya to train at altitude and won the South African Championships without dropping more than about four points in any set, winning the semi-final for the loss of four points and the final for the loss of another four.

I went through to the semi-final of the Australian Championships, again without dropping a set, and beat Dick Carter for the loss of nine or ten points in the quarter-final. When I was 2–0 up on Geoff Hunt in the semi-final and had a lead in the third it looked as if I was going through to the final of the Australian without losing a set; but then the tables were almost completely turned on me.

Geoff roared back into the match, as he is wont to do, and I only finally beat him 9–6 in the fifth. The following day, having hardly recovered, I had to take on a very vigorous Hiscoe, but just managed to beat him 9–1 in the fifth, thus, gaining my greatest triumph in 1968.

I had then in December to win the British Amateur, and dropped only one set to Mike Corby in a very good final. So 1968 was pretty good. It had regained me the No 1 position in the world because I had beaten Geoff Hunt and the other Australians. But at the same time there was a question mark about Nancarrow, who had beaten me afterwards in New Zealand in the autumn of that year, and, in my own mind, a considerable doubt about whether I could carry through a triumph in the World Championship. Even though I had had my most successful year, even though I was regarded again as No 1, the burden of responsibility was eroding my confidence.

In Perth, in August 1968, I was certain that I was better than those other people and that I was going to beat them regardless of how I felt when I went on that court. I was fiercely ambitious and determined to do this again in January and February 1969 but in the most critical stage of the whole 18 months my confidence seemed to waft away. It just seemed to disappear over a couple of months. I struggled through the British Amateur, producing a good match in the final against Corby, but I just wasn't with it in the British Open and completely flipped against Nancarrow in the semi-final.

I then blundered through the team series, winning against Geoff Hunt in the final match against Australia, 9–7 in the fifth, and struggling through against Jawaid. I beat him 10–8 in the fifth in the match with Pakistan, but had to save a match point which would have lost us the whole match against them. Finally I went down in the final of the World Amateur title to Geoff Hunt at a stage when I felt that I was marginally better than him. He, however, was clearly the master on the day and there could be no excuses.

I was quite adamant that I was going to turn professional regardless of whether I won or lost.

I had no money. Squash was obviously the way I was going to earn my living so without knowing what to do, where to go, I knew that I had to turn professional and somehow continue what I had done.

The aftermath of that defeat by Hunt was the worst that I have ever had to suffer.

It was just an appalling void. There seemed nothing. There seemed no point. All the value of the work, the effort, and the energy seemed to have disappeared overnight. And to no purpurpose. I was crushed by events and by people. I felt a grievous sense of injustice and bitterness and I hated all around me. Most people seemed delighted that I had been beaten; obviously this wasn't true although one or two, who should have known better, definitely showed that they were pleased that I had lost. I knew there was a certain feeling within the S.R.A. that it was a damned good thing that I had been beaten. I had built up to a pitch, and the reaction was so extreme that it seemed I could not recover for a long time. Had I not been helped through this passage by Derek Ibbotson and his wife, Madeline, and the Pickering family, Ron and Jean, I don't know what I would have done.

One or two other athletes, notably shot-putter Mike Lindsay, one evening at the Sportsman's Club in London, tried to ease my pain with a deluge of alcohol. They all tried to get me to unwind, to relax, to lose myself in thinking about various other things and then to build up the enthusiasm again.

I always remember at that time talking to Lynn Davies about the disappointment of defeat and coming second. It does not matter whether you are 64th or second, you have been beaten. You're not first. I know how he felt when Beaman had that extraordinary leap in Mexico in the summer of '68, how he didn't feel like jumping any more because he knew he couldn't win; how there seemed little point in trying for the silver or the bronze because he had not come for them. It was obvious that the gold had gone so he packed it in. But he should still have gone for the big jump—never quit. In my sport there is always a chance even when one is 8–0 down, but when this particular final was over I felt like stopping because it seemed hopeless. I had blown at the wrong time. My opponent raised his game just when it seemed Barrington was set on the path to victory. He produced his most disciplined squash at the right time and this is the mark of a very great player.

It wasn't my habit to blow at critical stages—rather the opposite. After training so hard I had missed the boat. I faced this awful chasm and I was really frightened of pitching myself into it. Yet I felt that I had hope, that the water was there, that it was deep enough and that I would swim.

A trip to South Africa was definitely on. I didn't particularly want to go because I would be constantly asked: 'Why were you beaten?' This is in fact what happened and I got sick of having to explain how I had lost the first game after a long lead, had managed to level, then lost the third, blown, and not won another point. That question. It was a nightmare.

Every night I dreamt not only about that match but about many other things. It was a period of my life when I would have liked to have gone into hibernation.

But I found my way back.

Mohammed Yasin, then the Pakistan No. 1, seen here in action during the 1970 British Open in Birmingham.

Abou Taleb (U.A.R.) had been regarded as invincible until Jonah beat him on the way to winning his first Open title.

Jonah and Aftab Jawaid (Pakistan) during the 1970 Open Final in Birmingham. Jawaid had won the English Amateur Championship three times until beaten by Jonah in 1967.

Cam Nancarrow (Australia) 'who funnily enough turned out to be the player who gave me more trouble than anyone'. Here in action against Sajiid Muneer of Pakistan, he remained Jonah's 'bogey' until 1969.

December 1971. Jonah and Geoff Hunt. Friends or foes?

February 1972. Jonah and Gogi Alauddin (Pakistan) in action during their semi-final of the Open Championships held in the new glass-walled court at Sheffield.

7

Second Impressions

Clive Everton

My second meeting with Jonah was in the restaurant of the Edgbaston Priory Club at the World Team Championships in Birmingham. Considering that I had met him only once nearly twelve months previously, I wouldn't have been surprised if he hadn't recognised me. In fact, he got up from the middle of his meal, came over to my table and settled at once into conversation. 'You get to know some people in half an hour and there are others you can't get to know in ten years,' he said sometime later.

He told me that the following month he was going to turn professional but that he had very little idea how he was going to organise his life other than that he was determined not to sink into an endless round of coaching engagements relieved only by one or two tournaments a year. His plan was to become the first travelling squash professional, playing in tournaments and exhibitions all over the world and taking only a carefully selected coaching engagements. He regarded his playing standard as all-important and was determined, in squash's amateur-orientated world, to create events in which he could compete if the various national associations themselves did not promote them.

This would clearly demand more time spent on organisation and administration than he could afford from his all-consuming playing and training programme. He also wanted his equipment contracts to be professionally negotiated and a publicity campaign to be mounted which would establish his name with the general public instead of merely with the then very limited squash public.

He wanted to be a superstar and could see no reason why the

top squash players should not earn the sort of money from endorsements and the sort of acclaim from the public which, say, tennis players took as a right. I agreed with him.

I was at that time beginning to diversify my news agency beyond journalism into certain aspects of sports promotion.

A journalist acquires a wide and various knowledge of how things tick but rarely has an opportunity to put this knowledge to any practical use. I had never seen myself as a sportsman's agent but the opportunity to play some part in directing events rather than merely recording them was too good to miss.

Undoubtedly, he could have placed his affairs in the hands of a longer established agency which already handled many top names but his fear was that he would not receive the special attention he required if he was only one sportsman—and not with very great earnings either—among many contracted to one organisation. He wanted to grow with his own organisation and challenge established ideas on what a squash player could or could not do rather than settle for the obvious but possibly more limited benefits which could be offered by an established agent.

Squash Rackets Promotions thus came into being, with me acting as Jonah's General Manager, planning with him and executing the creative side of the operation, and Tony Hughes, a squash enthusiast who has his own accountancy practice in Birmingham, master-minding the financial side and negotiating the details of Jonah's contracts, the first two of which were an equipment contract with Dunlops and an endorsement/technical advice contract with Banbury Squash Courts.

It later transpired that Jonah had already signed a contract for this book ('Oh yes, I think I did sign something') although he was very evasive when pressed actually to start work on it. ('It's too early. It isn't the right time.') Eventually, he agreed that we could not wait until everybody, including him, was dead merely in order to make an account of his career definitive.

Jonah's first professional engagement was a disaster. Not a simple disaster but a many-sided and intricate disaster.

The danger signs were hoisted well in advance. Before delegating the arrangement of such matters, Jonah had fixed a couple of exhibitions in Ireland—which was excellent—but was also committed to a recording in the B.B.C.'s Bristol studios of a programme in the 'One Man's Life' series which, through a combination of circumstances, had to be recorded the previous evening.

'I'll fly Bristol to Cork the next morning,' Jonah announced.

Well, actually there were no flights from Bristol to Cork, only London to Cork.

'Ah well, I'll get a train to London.'

Snag about that, Jonah, is that you'll have to catch one at 4 in the morning to get you there in time.

'Four o'clock?'

It was no good lending him a car because he has never learnt to drive. There was no help for it; someone had to drive him to Bristol and from there to London Airport.

Ann Jefferson, Squash Rackets Promotions' patient and good-natured secretary, volunteered to act as chauffeuse, so at least we were making progress.

Jonah was still in Huddersfield, where Derek Ibbotson had been encouraging him to hop up hills, and undergo other refined tortures, but Derek agreed to drive him to Sheffield station to entrain for Birmingham where Ann would meet him.

Even when Jonah missed the train in Sheffield things did not seem too bad in the light of Derek's offer to drive him to the Watford Gap Service Station on the M1. Ann would meet him there at 5 and would take him down to Brisol in time for a meal and a rehearsal prior to the recording.

At about 6 o'clock Ann, starting to fret a little at Jonah's non-arrival, joined a queue for the only available phone at Watford Gap. Perhaps Jonah had phoned the office with yet another change of plan?

After dealing with the first five callers, the telephone then broke down, as if with sheer fatigue, just as Ann had reached the status of first wicket down in the queue.

No help for it then but to sit tight, order her fifth cup of tea, and reflect that it was, after all, April 1st.

At 6.30, Jonah and Derek touched down.

'Let's have a cup of tea,' said Jonah. At this point Jonah noticed that he had left his rackets at the Ibbotsons'.

Jonah's expected time of arrival of 7.30 in Bristol thus became 9.30 actual arrival. Rehearsal and all but the briefest preliminary talk were dispensed with, a meal was eaten and Jonah's interview with Jeremy Carrad was recorded from 10.30 till midnight.

Back to the hotel and a solemn promise from the night porter—'the most famous in the West Country'—to call Jonah and Ann at 6·30. As the plane left London at 9.20, even this gave none too great a margin, but the famous night porter, giving us an insight into what he might be famous for, omitted to call them until 7.00.

Breakfast was hasty and unsatisfactory. Ann was brought a cup, a saucer, milk, toast and marmalade. Jonah, three floors below, awoke to tea, butter, a plate and a knife.

At 7.20 Ann's Spitfire was flashing towards London so fast that Jonah's normally aggressive passengership—he was a habit of bellowing 'Go!' or 'Charge!' just as one is approaching traffic lights which are changing to red—was superfluous.

In fact, Jonah dozed for much of the journey, bestirring himself only to bestow a furious V sign on a driver who blasted his horn as Ann overtook him.

At 9.17 our heroes reached the airport, dashed into the B.E.A. building with three minutes to spare—and found that the air ticket had not arrived.

No, no that was impossible. The computer could confirm that tickets had been booked. . . . What was that? The computer had broken down.

By this time the plane had gone.

Into the car, miraculously still where it had been unceremoniously left right outside the main entrance—and over to the Aer Lingus building.

The next plane was full but Ann put Jonah on the waiting list. Not anticipating any involvement with Jonah's affairs that day I was out of the office, so Ann rang Tony Hughes. Could he tell the Irish party meeting Jonah at Dublin that he had missed the plane and would be arriving later—at Shannon.

Breakfast was eaten as they waited for a cancellation; none came.

Back to B.E.A. That was the move.

But where was Ann's car?

'Is that the police? Do you have a Spitfire RWD 789G?'

'Yes'

'Where is it?'

'At the car compound. . . .'

'Could you deliver it. . . .?'

No, they couldn't.

Jonah, who has an unquenchable sense of style in all situations, hailed a taxi:

'B.E.A. Building.'

'But that's only 500 yards.'

'Yes, can you get us there?'

He could and did for what he clearly regarded as the very reasonable charge of five shillings.

On another waiting list again behind a couple of dozen vociferous Irish. Jonah, sinking deeper and deeper into his collar, was ready to concede defeat.

Ann, who had again phoned Tony who had again phoned Ireland, pleaded with the checking-in office!

'He's a squash professional . . . he's got to play in this match. . . .'

'Here you are. Don't let that lot' (gesturing towards the jolly Irishmen) 'know I've given you a pass.'

Jonah ran for it. Ann again phoned Tony who again phoned Ireland to tell them that splashdown would, in fact, be at . . .

Ann hailed a taxi. 'The car compound at. . . .'

No, the taxidriver would rather not take her to the car compound.

Bus part of the way, walk the rest.

Two very large policemen were haranguing one small, uncomprehending Pakistani who was nervously trying to placate them with his driving licence and certificate of insurance.

Ann retrieved her car for the again extremely reasonable sum of £4. 10s. od and drove home. Thank goodness, that was that.

Well, no, not exactly. The Chief Constable of Berkshire would be interested to know her version of two incidents at roundabouts near Newbury. Apparently, a lorry had been forced to stop and a third party, travelling behind, thought so strongly that he should have been offered right of way that he had complained to the good Chief Constable to this effect.

Since in these cases one is considered guilty until proved innocent, a plea of 'Guilty' was clearly the only course.

Which explains how Ann's licence received its one and only endorsement and why the expense account submitted—and honourably paid by Jonah—contained the two strange items:

To retrieving car from compound:	£4. 10s. od.
To fine for driving without reasonable consideration for other road users:	£10. os. od.

8

The Big Gamble—1969

Jonah Barrington

During my South Africa trip, it occurred to me that there was a possibility, if one moved in the right way, of getting the game wide open. I was very aware of the fact the South African administration, the one I knew best of all, was quite certain that Open squash must come and the sooner the better because otherwise it would be beset by the many problems which hindered tennis and other sports. It was better to clear the decks while the game was still small. South Africa would benefit because it would mean that more players would be prepared to put in a bit of coaching to gain a little financial return. This would be helpful and would mean the standard of squash would improve there. As it happened, what I was led to believe was the attitude of the S.A. officials was not reflected in their strange inability to vote for Open squash not only in 1970 at the Federation meeting in London but again in New Zealand in 1971. Put not thy faith in officials—especially in sport.

I had a glimmer of hope that my own country would favour Open squash, and possibly also Egypt, India and Pakistan because they have good professionals. This virtually left out only Australia and New Zealand. Australia are obviously opposed to Open squash for a variety of reasons. Australian sporting officials are like ostriches. When it suits them, they just plunge their heads into the sand and remain there. They are puritanical when it suits their cause, as was seen for so long in tennis and they have successfully retarded the game in Australia, because they have quite simply destroyed the incentive of those who would dearly like to teach and yet still compete at the highest level.

They are not really improving the playing standard while

other countries, which have fewer facilities but more coaches, are making advances. The Australians are world champions but they have relied completely on Hunt, Hiscoe, Nancarrow and Carter. There are young players behind them, but certainly not the real depth which one would expect. No real depth will be there until they are prepared to open the game and have more people doing full-time coaching. But the decision of Hunt and Hiscoe to turn professional in September, 1971, will not only give some opportunity for representative honours to other players but will also impel the Australian association to re-examine and re-appraise all levels of the Australian game.

When I returned to Britain I did stir it up a bit. I realised that if players could be players, it would mean that the professionals would have more competition, more opportunity, more incentive to remain in good training and to work. Whether there was more competition or not, I was determined to retain and improve upon my own playing standard. This meant that I must not undertake too much individual coaching.

The Times 2.10.69

BARRINGTON SPEAKS OF 'HYPOCRISY'

By Rex Bellamy

Squash Rackets Correspondent

Britain's leading squash rackets player, Jonah Barrington, who turned professional last February, said yesterday that there was 'enough information on a number of leading players in Britain to sink the whole amateur ship and its cargo of hypocrisy'. He considers the evidence even clearer overseas: 'In some overseas countries, a form of professionalism has been practised for years.'

Barrington added: 'I shall not hesitate to make use of this information if the Squash Rackets Association and the International

Squash Rackets Federation are completely intractable on this matter.' He wants open squash—an abolition of the distinctions between amateurs and professionals—as quickly as possible. 'Britain can show the way,' he said.

Barrington discussed the issue yesterday afternoon with John Horry, secretary of the S.R.A. and I.S.R.F., who told him that the I.S.R.F. could make no decision until their next meeting, in New Zealand in 1971. Barrington thinks a personal vote would be justified—'or more players will be taking more money'.

In addition to the pressure from Barrington himself, it is expected that his country (Ireland), his county (Cornwall), and his club (Lansdowne) will all provoke urgent thinking by selecting Barrington for their respective teams. In addition, the S.R.A. 'amateur status' sub-committee are considering their report on the same issue.

Though Barrington may be the catalyst (by no means an unusual role), the important thing is that the question of making squash an open game should be assessed entirely on its own merits. The game has boomed to such an extent in recent years that there have inevitably been many abuses of the rules concerning amateur status: and there will be more until the game becomes open.

I had been considering throughout the South African winter of 1969 the beauty of playing a series with Geoff Hunt. First, I wanted to have the mightiest opposition in the world to pit my wits against. What better way was there to improve my own game in the long term.

Secondly, it could also, in the long term, be financially beneficial. I thought that perhaps Geoff could be persuaded to come to Britain for the Open, which with his presence might regain its former status of being the top title in the world.

I decided to pay his return fare from Australia and guarantee him the amateur maximum of £8 a day expenses for a six weeks' visit.

The tour was a spectacular success. I had my doubts initially. I wondered about my own play. I suffered from a nightmare at first that there would be no financial return, but this became a secondary thought because the playing side of it was so much the most important thing for me. No doubt the money side will grow in importance as the years go by but at that time I had more fears about my playing ability. Although I had trained hard, I had the usual feeling that something might go wrong.

As it turned out, this experiment of the series was worth a pot of gold—a pot of gold from the financial aspect because in the long run it will probably bring us an enormous amount of money through the experience we have gained and the developments which must accrue. It was a pot of gold on the playing side because although I was beaten, and beaten well, it provided me with a new incentive, new targets, and made me realise that one must always work because one will never be too good: one will be good but never good enough. There is always a need and room for improvement so one cannot stand still. I reacted in the right way.

Bringing Geoff Hunt over was a purely personal thing and yet there were at least two associations who could have helped: the Australian and my own. But they were not prepared to do anything to aid this project. Some in high places privately scoffed that we would never get the tour off the ground. In fact, we fixed fifteen venues in eight days of phone calls: the whole tour was set up in four weeks.

I always had misgivings because I am not the most confident of people, regardless of what other people may think. I never forget the possibility that there is another player better than me and that I may be beaten. As it turned out Geoff Hunt was playing better than I was during the months of November, December and January.

I trained harder than I have ever trained before, although much of this was done off the court or on the court without a ball; but despite a negligible amount of competition, I still felt that, physically, I was wonderfully prepared for him and because I knew this, I was mentally in good shape.

Such self-assurance as I had was soon rudely shattered. Geoff began particularly well by destroying me 3–0 in 40 minutes in the first match at Coventry. I lost a five-setter at

Northwood in the second encounter and went down in the two following matches both in four, so when I came to the British Open I was 4–0 down with eleven to go.

Geoff made the fatal error in the first seven or eight minutes of the Open final letting me get a long lead: he tried to hit the ball too hard and too low, and I was 7–1 up before he started to tighten up. He pulled right back but, as was absolutely vital, I got that game and the match had to go to four sets. The first few minutes cost him dearly.

We then toiled on. He tightened up in the second, found his best length in that game and pinned me at the back. I started to lose my length. He was cutting my shots off and worked me right round the court. I started to get very tired not because I was unfit but because he was moving me at a very fast pace, and I had trained to play at a slower pace for an extended period. He was taking me round at a four-minute-mile pace when I had come prepared for 10,000 metres. The pace went on through the second and the third as he dominated the centre of the court and made no mistakes. There was an inevitability about the eventual outcome.

In the fourth, he led again but Nasrullah had come down at the end of the third and given me the golden advice that I was hitting too short and that it was better for me to overhit than underhit. In that fourth game, I decided that, unlike in the World Amateur final, when I made mistakes and lost the fourth set 9–0, I would not go for a single stroke out of hand unless I had a really excellent position, and that I would not give him one single point. He would have to win every single point, I would not make any errors. He led about 3–1 but the rallies were getting longer. In the middle of that game, at about 3–4, he suddenly slowed down and seemed unable to take the ball so much on the volley. If I could keep my head I could keep my pace going, but Geoff was beginning to founder. I won the fourth and the fifth. I knew again that if I returned the ball, played it sensibly away from him when I was out of hand he would not come back into the match. The match took about

2 hours 12 minutes. We were both shattered. At the end he suffered from cramp and I just felt awfully tired through the mental hammering I had taken in trying to play the bitter war of attrition for almost an eternity. The chinks in Geoff's armour rarely appear and then don't show up too clearly.

It took me a long time to get over that match but Geoff must have felt absolutely destroyed because he must have realised that, had he not played so carelessly in the first game, he would have won.

Afterwards he won another nine matches in the series and I only won two. Overall, he was playing better, much more consistently, much more aggressively; he'd taken his game to a higher level than I had and it was only on the one occasion when I had to resort to all my powers of concentration and draw out the last reserves of determination that I could overcome him.

The lesson to me was that I had to change my game fundamentally, take more on the volley, be more aggressive and not be such a puppet on a string. Instead of being too confined I would allow myself to flow, to get control over the centre of the court and to quicken up. That was why I spent the whole of 1970 trying to speed up my game regardless of a loss of control.

Geoff Hunt is very close to me in the capacity to come back after taking punishment. A number of players will come back for a while and then fade and that will be the end of it, whereas Geoff will keep coming back and coming back. This is why our matches are extraordinary. We punish each other to an unbelievable extent. I have the greater reserves of stamina over a sustained period; he has a great talent for putting in fiery bursts and setting a pace that no player can stay with. I can't maintain that pace for a long period of time although I can play for a longer period of time at my own pace, so it was a case of trying to keep him there till he came back to my pace and then fell below it.

Technically he was a far better player than me. He employed a far wider range of strokes; he was far less confined than I was in his thinking. It was doubted by some members of the press that I would ever find my way back against this much younger opponent, but the series merely provided a springboard for me to get to a higher level, because I put what I had learned from him in to immediate practice.

9

Going Home

Clive Everton

At the end of the tour, the sense of anticlimax was so prodigious that I was amazed at the self-discipline with which Jonah pushed himself straight into the drudgery of an even more gruelling training schedule. He was edgy; he was irritable; he had more time to devote to long-term prospects—and even less inclination.

But as Jonah and I drove from London to Cornwall, he was looking forward to a visit home as he always did after a few weeks in the claustrophobic, subterrannean world of the Lansdowne, his London headquarters on the edge of Berkeley Square.

He has shared a number of flats but currently he was with his sister, Geraldine, off Kensington Church Street. When in London he eats either at the club or 'down the alley' in one of the tiny snack-bars in Lansdowne Row across the road. He does his weight-training in the Mayfair Gymnasium in Paddington Street—again walking distance from the club—and his running training in Green Park—which is only running distance.

For weeks on end, when he sacrifices public engagements for the all-embracing discipline of his training schedule, he has remained on this tight, self-created island. He does not socialise at all. The nearest he gets to self-indulgence is watching an hour's television at the end of the day when he is so tired that it is a major effort to get out of his chair and go to bed.

When he has no immediate external target, like a series of matches or a championship, all his energies are channelled inwards. Frustrated by the lack of opportunity to display his talent publicly, he can only pit himself against a self-defined perfection in an obsessive drive towards a daily marginal improvement in fitness, control and knowledge.

It is at these times when inhumanly hard work leads to no commensurate satisfaction that Jonah is most likely to be irritable, on edge or despondent that a variety of promotional projects are not proceeding quickly enough.

So on such a flying visit to Cornwall he was like a schoolboy being released for the holidays. The further we travelled out of London, the more he relaxed, the more freely light-hearted reminiscence and gossip flowed.

'This was the corner where I always used to try to hitch a lift. I used a cunning ploy once when I was with a girl. She did the thumbing and when a car stopped I popped out from behind the hedge to join her. Not original but bloody effective.'

By the time we'd got through Exeter, he was in high spirits.

'I think a phone call to my mother is indicated,' he said. 'I'll warn her that we'll be arriving about nine o'clock, won't we?'

'What a dutiful son you are.'

'Ah well, it's not just that. If I ring now, the old meal will be ready when we get there.'

Suddenly we were off the main road, winding off down a labyrinth of country lanes through which he piloted me with the native's sureness of touch.

'Next right. Next left. Next right.'

'Are we still in England?'

'I'm taking you a short cut, next right.'

Peals of laughter lasting intermittently all the way to Morwenstowe. 'Next right' had, in fact, been a large field.

The lanes got narrower and narrower. Suddenly we couldn't go any further because there was a farm gate in the way.

'Here we are.'

I parked the car in the yard just away from the outbuildings, which, when Jonah's father had been alive, had housed a few pigs and chickens.

'There's one thing: if you ever wanted to hide, nobody would ever find you here.' This judgement had been substantiated by a boy friend of Geraldine's who, many years before, had journeyed down to see her.

'He arrived in the area at 11.30 and I could hear him circling round in his car till he finally found us at 2.30.'

Yet the isolation of 'Marratons,' the Barringtons' home, had been a positive influence on Jonah's development.

'One of the reasons why Nicholas and Jonah played together so much was that there weren't many other things they could do,' said Mrs. Barrington as she sewed a button on to Jonah's Great Britain blazer. 'They weren't brought up to expect to go to the pictures or things like that although they both made up for this' (illicitly) 'while they were at Cheltenham.

'The boys got on extremely well although they fought over everything as boys always do. They started playing table tennis on the nursery table; that's where Jonah got his quickness.

'All their games were competitive. We had the most marvellous cycle track here and there were endless games of football on the lawn.

'My husband didn't lean over backwards to help them at all. I don't think Jonah's success is anything to do with anything my husband and I did. It's something in Jonah's nature. He's a leader—both boys are.

'Even as a small boy, Jonah always knew what he wanted. If you gave him a choice, he would always have a preference. He would never say he didn't mind.

'He was a very truthful child. He knew that if he told the truth he wouldn't be punished.

'If he was given a bar of chocolate or some sweets he would always bring me a piece of that chocolate or a sweet.

'Jonah always had to be level with Nicholas. He was always putting on Nicholas's shoes instead of his own because they were bigger.

'Nicholas went to school two years before Jonah and Jonah was very impatient to go to school to catch up with him.

'He came home from his first day at school bitterly disappointed. He said: "I thought they were going to teach me to read but all they did was show me how to thread beads."'

'He was always determined about anything he wanted to do. The boys had a routine at one time of playing outside until "Dick Barton" came on the radio.

'Once Nicholas nipped inside, locked the door and teased Jonah by rattling the door from inside. Jonah was so furious that he stuck his fist through the window and partially severed an artery.

'It was lucky the doctor was only two miles away or it could have been very serious. There was half a washbasin of blood. This was when Jonah was six.

'My mind didn't take in that Jonah might achieve anything special until about a year before the first big thing he won. My husband would say: "But there's nothing in it. There's no money in it. What's he going to do?"

'Had he lived I'm sure he would have been incredibly thrilled by Jonah's M.B.E. I think part of Jonah's driving force had come from a sense of guilt at having not done so well at Trinity.

'I think the worst thing my husband ever did was to allow him to go to Trinity when he was only 17. He could have gone to a crammer, got more A's and walked into either Oxford or Cambridge.

'I think Jonah pushes himself very hard. If anything, he expects too much of himself. I don't think it's good for anyone to be under constant strain as he is.

'There are too many pressures. That's why I worry so much about him. I feel he should be able to relax more. In some ways, it's a pity he's not married.

'He went through a bad time but I never allowed myself to think that he would be a drop-out or a misfit. So many young men of Jonah's type go for a long time finding their level.

'Naturally I'm very proud of him—I'm proud of all my children. Locally they talk about the honour he's brought to the area.

In the village now I'm not Major Barrington's wife any more: I'm Jonah's mother.'

She applied herself studiously to Jonah's blazer again.

'He's rough on his clothes.' She sewed for a second or two. 'What are you calling this book?'

'The Book of Jonah.'

'Perhaps they'll give it away as Sunday School prizes.'

10

Bouncing Back—1970

Jonah Barrington

In the last match of the tour, in Dublin, Geoff had beaten me 9–5, 9–2, 9–3. I wrote in my diary: 'Geoff really showed his mastery particularly on a cold court with the Aussie ball. He has shown the way during this series and I must set about improving many aspects of my game, particularly the following:

1. General technique in striking the ball. I must concentrate on more fire power to a length and short, particularly when hitting off the wrong foot. The wrist must remain up 99% of the time. *Must* get racket back earlier behind the head and swing well and through, not round my body.
2. General technique in stepping in on the ball, hitting on the volley, the half-volley and on the rise. Should make my toes very sore when stamping down. Continuous volley attack when playing but must strike a length before cutting off to the front with (a) straight stroke, drop volley or drive (b) volley boast, not too low as long as taken really early and to sit up on the T position. (c) ordinary boast—angle as before, N.B. These strokes are kills. Volley practice with another player so necessary and practise on one's own religiously every day.
3. General condition. Still getting tired. Unable to sustain attack. Must concentrate on interval work on court and the running and weight training; to be well prepared by at least 20 minutes warm-up either on the court or in open doing some strides and sprints before every match.

It's easier to learn from defeats than wins because limitations show that much more clearly, so far from being downcast I felt re-motivated. I got stuck into a new schedule: On February 4th, for instance, I ran 4 miles between 8.30 and 9.00. did court practice from 10.30 to 11.30, played from 11.30 to 12.15, did interval training from 12.20 to 12.40 and weight training from 5.30 to 7.00. Only in so far as I did not play again in the afternoon or evening was this an untypical day.

Next day, I roared out into Green Park and ripped a leg muscle, the first injury of my career that I'd had in training. I was unable to play from February 5 until February 21, a very long break for me, and it was uncertain whether I could accept an invitation to go to Pakistan for their Open Championship. I reacted by doing a tremendous amount of weight training and pressure training in the boiler room of the Lansdowne.

On February 15, I wrote: 'Good session but would do anything for some good old squash and running.'

The previous day, I had been to a Rugby International with my mate from behind the food counter, Ronski, and our friend, Jim Nolan, and decided that it was time for total relaxation.

I went on the booze. That night, taking my daily reading, I recorded 'No pulse!'

'Muscle seems to be starting to mend,' I wrote next day—perhaps shocked by the excess of the night before.

Pakistan set their Championship back for a week and even so I went there not properly prepared, something I shouldn't have done. Just before I left on March 7th I wrote: 'Am gradually finding my feet again. Making slight improvement on backhand wing. Nothing to offer on forehand. Grip keeps slipping. Stamping is useful but pointless all the time. Will go steady in Pakistan and really rip into training after the Championship.'

On my first day in Pakistan, I played Naz's nephew Torsam—Roshan's son—and he beat me 3–0. I felt very puffed and out of sorts, but by the time the tounament started on March 12, I was playing better. I beat Jehan 3–0 in the quarters, professional champion Yasin 3–1 in the semis (winning the two tough first games 9–7, 9–6) and then Jawaid 3–1 in the final, losing the third and just managing to hang on in the fourth.

The following day, my leg muscle was sore. I started an exhibition tour with Aftab, but it was very soon apparent that my leg had gone.

I had an immense amount of treatment during the three-week tour and it gradually healed. More important, I had a fortuitous meeting with Mr. Durrani, the managing director of Pakistan International Airlines, with whom I seemed to strike up an immediate rapport. While discussing my hopes for the future of squash, I talked about forming a circus of players and the obstacles relating to it.

He immediately dealt with the major obstacle of financing air travel by suggesting that P.I.A. might fly the players London–Tokyo–London free of charge. At that moment the first Barrington Circus was born. Aftab Jawaid did an immense amount of the background work and later in the year we were able to carry out our plan.

Meanwhile, I returned to Britain with Aftab via Teheran, all the time paying constant attention to technique and conditioning. By the end of April I was very happy with the way many things were going on the playing side.

In the early part of May, I made an offer to Taleb for the tour but in general this was a quiet month. I made one of my rare visits home where I amazed my mother with violent movements around the yard lashing out at imaginary balls. She was now quite convinced that madness had finally set in and that there was no need for a second opinion.

We pressed on with setting up our tour which we were tying in with the Australian Professional Championships at the end of August, which carried a $1,000 first prize.

I was unhappy with my training during June and July but felt that if I could keep up my court schedule something would come—at least the work was being put in.

Open squash was turned down at a Federation meeting in

London on July 21 and a few days later Taleb and I, together with Sharif Khan, who had come over from Canada to join us, left for the tour.

The tour went on from the middle of August until January 24 with breaks for the British Open in December and the British Amateur in January. We didn't have the full party throughout the tour and we had changes as well.

We set out from London and stopped in Karachi for a meeting with P.I.A. executives to settle the final details. The idea was that Jawaid would join Sharif, Taleb and myself in Australia about two weeks before we set out on the major part of the tour, under the auspices of P.I.A. The fifth-ranked Australian amateur, Rainer Ratinac, was to be the fifth member of our group.

As it happened Jawaid didn't join us until Manila, where he had most efficiently arranged the promotion in all the newspapers and on television, so it was just the three musketeers, Taleb, Barrington and Khan, that travelled so extensively throughout New South Wales after the Australian Professional Championship. I won that title at some cost, because Sharif was beaten in the quarter-final and Taleb in the semi-final by an Australian called Tony Hosford.

Because it was obvious that I was the favourite to win we had settled that we would share the proceeds, but the pressure was suddenly all on me because the other two had lost. Fortunately I was able to get past Hosford 3–0 in the final. I don't think he'd played against my sort of game before and he found me a little more persistent than the other two. We thus made off with the 1,000 dollars prize, the largest from any competition in the world at that time and a very fine effort by the Australian professionals who arranged it.

After that we moved into a very long tour of New South Wales which had been arranged with the New South Wales professional body. During this tour we suffered the roughest part of what had already been a fairly unsatisfactory Australian winter: there in the wilds in the worst floods which had hit that area for about forty years were Taleb, Barrington and Khan, plus an Australian professional, Haydon Daly, who was trying to keep our headlights above the water.

We played on twenty-seven successive nights, at the end of which I had to fly down to Melbourne for the Australian Open, which had been arranged at very short notice during the championships in Sydney at the end of August.

These exhibition evenings used to go on for about three and a half hours but it seemed longer. We whizzed around from court to court desperately trying to keep the galleries entertained and usually ended up with a performance in which I played against two of the others, Sharif and Taleb, or Sharif and the Australian pro. This usually went down very well because all of us were keen on trying a thing or two. We played one sudden-death set, American scoring. Sudden death was truly the name of the game because the tripping, hacking and boring that went on would have served us well in an Australian Rules football match. It was very hard work with very little sleep and an enormous amount of travelling in cars provided by our sponsors. At the end of it, the boys were on the thin dividing line between being prepared for the Open Championship and being flat on their faces. This is a very narrow margin and I was fortunate to get through the first round against Ray Lewis, No 3 or 2 in Victoria, who led me 2–1 and 7–6 in the fourth. I was very sluggish and once he realised that I was not functioning too well he played better and better.

Thirty-six hours before that match I had played, on a Saturday night, in a 3-hour series of matches in Sydney. On the Sunday morning that was a 6 o'clock start in order to catch a plane to Melbourne, where I had a TV and radio interview before flying back to Syndey on the 1.15 plane. That night I had another series of matches in Sydney which ended at about 11 p.m. and were duly followed by another early call for the trip to Melbourne. Worse, when we got to the airport at 7.30 on Monday morning, the three musketeers found that there were no tickets for them. Someone had blundered. We were at

Sydney Airport for four hours trying to fix things and didn't get a plane until nearly 11.30.

We arrived in Melbourne at lunch time and late that afternoon I went on court against Ray Lewis. It was soon apparent that if ever I was going to crack up this would have been the day. In fact, as I have indicated, I was very lucky and just managed to pull through. Sharif beat Rainer Ratinac 10–9 in the fifth, a good performance as Rainer is always a difficult person to get by; but Taleb struggled and went down to Lionel Robards, a barrister who has been one of the top Australians for about five or six years now. That I went through to win this title was probably the greatest achievement of my career, because I didn't feel that I had the ideal background training before the tour that I would have liked, although I had better practice with Sharif and Taleb than I would otherwise have had.

In the second round, which was the quarter-final, I was determined to get really stuck in against Doug Stephenson, the Australian No 5. In fact I was leading him 9–0, 8–1 when something pretty horrible happened. I don't know to this day what it was. At 8–1 in the second, with Stephenson fading rapidly, I suddenly felt I couldn't breathe. Everything started to spin and I just leant against the wall. I had to continue playing and two minutes later the score was 8–8, then the game was his 10–8 and one minute later I was on my knees outside the court. A doctor came down and my pulse was going about 400 m.p.h. After about a minute of this the doctor tried to get me into the changing rooms but I realised that if I stayed out of the court for more than a minute that would be the end of the match. So I dragged myself on court again and started to play. Fortunately I was playing the one Australian with an humanitarian streak because he didn't drive the nails into my coffin as he should have done. Gradually my legs came back to me and, even though I felt tremendous discomfort in my side, I managed to win the next two sets and the match and get back to the hotel for a long rest.

I felt very unwell, as if I had one hell of a strain in the side around the heart, and I went through a whole host of tests the following day which thankfully proved negative.

I still had two matches to go. In the semi-final I had to play Lionel Robards who, fortunately for me, had beaten Cam Nancarrow in the quarter-final. I have beaten Cam since then but I always feel slightly uncomfortable before playing him because we never have a very attractive game and because he has turned me over on too many occasions for me to feel too much confidence.

Lionel I managed to take out 3–1. I played fairly quietly but won clearly. On the other side, Hiscoe ran Hunt to five sets so at least he had been under a bit of pressure. This competition was played over four days so there were none of those great long gaps that we have in our tournaments over here.

On the fourth night, Hunt and Barrington therefore fronted up against each other for the first time since the British Open final. I must say that I did not feel too confident of success but planned to play as comfortably as I could to start with, to pace myself a little to see how my breathing was and hope that he would give me just a little bit of a start, as he had in the British Open a few months earlier.

This is exactly what he did do because he made six mistakes in the first seven rallies. I went to 7–0 and had that game in my pocket without using too much energy. This was a priceless advantage to me and I feel now that Geoff again lost the match in that first game. Through losing it he committed himself to playing at least four games if he was to win. As it turned out, he stepped up the pace in the second, played much better and much more positively. Sure enough, it was one set all and for two-thirds of the third game it was very much Hunt with Barrington struggling to stay in the match.

It looked as if Hunt was going straight through him 3–1.

Then, towards the end of the third, Geoff began to tire. He was also struck by my racket on the backswing but I don't think this had any effect on the result of the match. The cut that he had on the eye did not affect his vision in any way although the blood that ran down the side of his face made him look like some battered pug, particularly as he wouldn't clean it off. Every time I went to serve and looked across at him I would see this baleful bloody eye staring back.

Geoff was starting to labour and even though he got that third game I really picked up the pace at the beginning of the fourth and started to take the centre of the court completely away from him. From then on it was a case of playing very sensibly, competently taking the ball on the volley as much as possible, not doing anything too dramatic or too spectacular but gradually grinding him into the dirt. In the middle of the fifth game he got cramp in one of his legs so that he was actually standing like a stork at times.

I asked him whether he was okay and he said he was, so I served quickly a couple of times to add a couple more points and finally managed to hole out.

It is very difficult to tell the tale of these matches in words. It is a bit like a 15-round contest for the middle-weight championship of the world; a couple of men firing salvos off at each other again and again. First, one has the other down and then the other gets on top until, in the end, one gradually gains a partial supremacy on the particular night. It would be appalling if we had to play each other every day although it would be interesting to see who finally didn't get out of bed.

The winning of the Australian Open title, which incidentally was sponsored by Vigorade, a product with which the great athlete Ron Clarke was connected, meant that I had set the seal competitively on a very good tour of Australia. Vigorade provided a tremendous amount of incentive to pros through the prize money and thus initiated a trend which will be very beneficial to the Australian game.

Sharif bowled along happily to take the second professional prize and Taleb managed to nail Hosford on the final night, just before I played my match with Geoff. He won 9–7 in the fifth in a struggle that was particularly appreciated by the packed gallery. So the boys came out of that tournament feeling a bit more chirpy. All we had to do now was to finish the rest of the series of one-night stands starting with a few exhibitions around Victoria with Tony Hosford in early October.

We had quite a lot of fun on this part of the tour, that is except for Tony, who suffered from a series of physical disorders from boils on his bum to a nasty dose of 'flu. But he took all this with great humour and instead of taking a rest on a couple of nights, which he should have done, played every night even though, from day to day, we wondered whether he was going to survive till morning. We continued our *pièce de resisantce* at the end of the evening when I played Tony and one of the others. Sharif or Abou and I would virtually play a singles, with criminal injustices being perpetrated on each other's bodies, punctuated by fantastic arguments with a hapless referee who had not been warned that the whole thing was a hoax. This, I fear, often found us in far better humour at the end than the referee. This classic pattern would every now and then be interrupted by a figure flying up the court. This was neither Barrington, Sharif or Taleb so who was it? We stopped to ask the wise referee; who on earth was this man who had decided to interfere in our singles? Whereupon we were told that this was the noted Australian, Tony Hosford, who had gathered all his resources after a five-minute rest for a desperate lunge up the court after the ball.

Tony has a lot of potential, but his fatal flaw is that he likes to smoke the odd cigarette. He is very fast, a good striker of the ball and was a promising junior who didn't come on as rapidly as he should have done. Nevertheless, I feel that he will be a considerable danger to the top Australians if he is given the opportunity to have a crack at them and, more important, if he decides to put a bit of work in.

I must recall one other incident when we were playing our two against one, on this occasion with Taleb. Suddenly the door opened and four figures raced on dressed in Arab costume, grabbing Taleb and hustling him out of the court. Taleb wasn't quite the same boy for a few days afterwards even though it was soon apparent that they were just some of our friends in Victoria who had decided they were going to give Taleb a bit of a rave.

We were travelling with a degree of accord but there were very considerable difficulties even with three of us. The main problem was that I was the No 1 player and the manager as well. These two don't go together. If I'd been the No 1 player, the manager *and* ten years older the position would have been different in that I would have been able to crack the whip a bit but it is particularly difficult to crack the whip at somebody who has also climbed Everest. Taleb was the greatest player in the world when I came into the game and you can't crack the whip over a former world champion. As the tour of Australia neared its end, we became aware that we were going to have many difficulties in co-ordinating with P.I.A. as there seemed to be little go within the P.I.A. organisation apart from Mr. Durrani, the managing director, and Aftab Jawaid; everyone we dealt with was incapable of making a decision. We had problems fixing up the clothing for the tour. We had to wear P.I.A. blazers and thin trousers. We had decided not to get the trousers in Sydney, but I set up the making of the blazers only to find the block for the crests hadn't arrived from Pakistan. Had we not been delayed at Sydney Airport for a couple of hours en route for Manila we would have travelled away from Sydney without the crest; but fortunately the plane arrived just before we headed out, so we travelled to the Philippines with our blazer badges ready to be put on there.

Jawaid met us in Manila, the first efficiency we had seen for quite some time. We had a terrific reception, even though we were only in transit, and we eagerly awaited our return from Tokyo a few days later. We now had the full complement as Rainer Ratinac had joined us in Australia after threats from the Australian Association that they would take away his amateur status if he joined my group. This, in fact, they did.

The Barrington Circus was at last on the way. Initially things weren't too bad although from the outset Jawaid and Taleb, not the best of friends, were waiting for every opportunity to stick knives into each other. Jawaid was in a better position to do this because he was managing a lot of the administration and Taleb was merely one of the players with no responsibilities at all. Jawaid was the top man and Taleb didn't like this. There was already constant friction between them and in Tokyo, outside our playing time, Taleb spent most of the time on his own, which was very unsatisfactory. After the tour was over I felt that I never wanted to tour again with top players. I felt that they were very selfishly there for just one big pay day and not to develop the whole touring concept. It was a pioneering plan and everyone in it had to realise that, although they would be getting a dividend, it was a stepping stone for the future for each and every one of us.

The tour was a mixture of success and failure. Success came to a spectacular degree in Japan where there were only three squash courts. We played at the British Embassy and at Yokohama. We were also scheduled to play at Kobe but instead had played twice at the British Embassy. There were cocktail parties; we met the press; we had some films taken; we met Japanese business-men; and we triggered off what will turn out to be the largest expansion in squash in any country since the explosion in Australia in the late 50's and early 60's. In our tour of Japan we showed the game at the highest level to the right sort of people. In terms of the future this was the high point.

We didn't see much of Japan although we saw enough to discover that it was the most expensive country we had visited. All the players were quite pleased to get on the P.I.A. plane to head back to Manila. We were given appalling treatment by the P.I.A. officials in Tokyo and it became even more apparent to me than before that, apart from Mr. Durrani not one P.I.A. official was interested in what we were doing and some thought the venture absolutely pointless. In Manila we had an enormous amount of publicity. We were on TV; we were in every newspaper, every day, morning and evening and superficially it was a fantastic visit. There was one court at the Manila Boat Club which had recently been constructed—mostly at the instigation of an Australian. For us the pleasant surroundings included the most beautiful girls in greater numbers than I have seen anywhere else in the world. This made me feel better, but the sober reality was that success could only be superficial because the Philippines consists of a few rich and an awful lot of poor. And I have always said that in no country which is not essentially middle class can squash be really big.

The game of squash did not benefit to the same extent from our visit to the Philippines as it did from that to Japan, and the same applied at our next stop, Bangkok, where we suffocated at the airport for over an hour while we experienced more P.I.A. inefficiency. Dressed in our blazers and team trousers in a terminal which was not air-conditioned, we found the sweat dribbling down our backsides. All the boys were most uncomfortable and starting to become irritable, when finally we were saved and taken outside for a photograph to be taken. Through all the sweat and irritation we managed the most incredible smiles of joy and glee. In the papers the following day it said that the prophet (me) had arrived with his band of disciples. Another comment was that I looked like John the Baptist coming out of the wilderness. It was here that we met the incredible Anton Perrera, sports editor of the *Bangkok Times,* a great squash enthusiast. It was due to him that we had more coverage in a national newspaper than I have ever seen before. There were front pages and inner profiles; Abou Taleb came out as the wizard Merlin and Sharif Khan, with a scimitar in his hand, was the reincarnation of Ghengis Khan. Members of the Bankgok Sports Club looked after us exceptionally well and there were again superb females walking to the right and left of us.

With three countries visited, things looked pretty good although P.I.A. were getting nought out of ten for their help. Jawaid was getting ten out of ten for covering up their mistakes and managing to get the whole show off the ground. The boys were turning in some incredible stuff on the court and we were getting the right sort of publicity; but if Japan was a real success story and Manila and Bangkok were at least superficial successes, from here the graph went down and down.

We flew from Bangkok to East Pakistan. East Pakistan, at the best of times, is a depressing country and was now about to suffer its worst and most terrifying hours. The people have no opportunities at all. There is a sharper divorce from the West Pakistanis than the Indians; they didn't look like the West Pakistanis, they didn't want the West Pakistanis, and the P.I.A. officials there, Bengalis, certainly didn't want Aftab Jawaid. We played in Dacca and Chittagong where the temperatures were very high and the social side non-existent. This depressed us, Taleb most of all. We didn't feel that we wanted to spend three weeks in Pakistan but were committed to do so.

Rainer Ratinac was suffering from stomach trouble and a series of minor irritations was getting us down. We were in East Pakistan for only five or six days but that was enough to really unsettle us and provide me with enough evidence to realise that something pretty horrible was going to happen there. I didn't expect a cyclone to hit East Pakistan five days after we left but I could envisage civil disorder. There could have been no way in which East Pakistan could have continued to have been bled of the resources by the West Pakistanis. The latter, in my book, have been guilty of cold, calculated murder.

We went into West Pakistan to the home of the game's greatest players, the Khans. Sharif was going home for the first time for 13 years and was as much a foreigner as me. In fact, I think the country frightened him more than it frightened anyone else. The boys were now under pressure. Taleb could find no outlet to amuse himself. There was more and more friction between him and Jawaid; Sharif was desperately on edge because he wanted to put on a good show for the relatives he had in Peshawar. I had the most extraordinary match with him in one exhibition in which he stole a march on me. I wanted him to play well in front of his own people but I felt that having let him in the match he rapidly disposed of me in a way which made me look rather silly. As I was the Australian and British Open Champion, I felt that he had let me down. I had a hell of a row with him so, one way or another, the tour was coming to a grinding halt.

Compromises were made. We struggled through Lahore with Taleb psychologically at his lowest ebb but finished on a reasonable note in Karachi. It was only when we reached Rawalpindi, that we were finally received really well by P.I.A. officials. There were a couple of sportsmen involved in P.I.A. at Rawalpindi who obviously felt that they wanted to do something for us and we were immensely grateful to them.

Because of them the tour started to improve and the hospitality in Lahore was tremendous. The father of a young international, Sajjad Muneer, is the Chairman of the Central Zone association there and had organised matters so that we could have no grumbles at all.

The programme after Pakistan was that we should travel to Teheran to play exhibitions for four days and then fly back to London where we would complete the P.I.A. tour with a special evening at the Lansdowne.

We could then start our own individual preparations for the British Open Championship which was to start about a week later, in Birmingham.

The difficulties remained: Abou Taleb's wife had had a baby and he badly wanted to see her. He was very miserable, very depressed, and I decided that it would be an excellent idea for him to go off to Cairo for three or four days and then fly back to London to join us for the final P.I.A. night at the Lansdowne Club.

Abou duly left, much more cheerful because he was going home and because he had been paid quite a considerable sum of money.

The four of us continued to play in Teheran where we were well looked after by Mike Hill and Nigel Faulks. We struggled through our matches—'struggled' because Rainer Ratinac and I went through an immense amount of court training in the mornings with the British Open very much in our thoughts. We were looking forward to getting to London, and more precisely to our Birmingham headquarters, the Jefferson Arms, Solihull. To me it was like going home because I could rest up and be completely at ease in surroundings where Mr. and Mrs. Jefferson were amazingly tolerant of my peculiar nature.

When the four of us eventually arrived in London, there was a press conference at the Lansdowne Club at which I told the press that something pretty dramatic was going to happen in Japan. I emphasised again that in any middle-class country the game would develop. But there was one unhappy note: Abou Taleb had not appeared for this final P.I.A. engagement at the Lansdowne.

Fortunately, Philip Ayton and Paul Millman came in to provide a third match. Taleb didn't appear for the British Open and the first we heard of him was a telephone call about December 18th saying that he had arrived back in England. By that time I had already brought in Mohammed Yasin, the Pakistani No 1 professional, for the Benson and Hedges section of the tour which was a ten-venue series throughout Britain.

The Taleb story is a constant source of disappointment to me because I consider him to have been the greatest player of the 1960's decade, certainly one of the greatest of all time, and not too old to find his way back into the game. I felt that this was a golden opportunity for him to work with a group or players of a high standard and to find the fitness that he required to make himself a big name again. Instead of finding this an incentive, all that happened was that he reacted to Jawaid's goading and was in a way psychologically squashed. He actually lost a lot of his quality during that tour. I think that was, to a certain extent, my fault; I think I should have cossetted him a bit more than I did. I could have been a bit cleverer in keeping him away from Jawaid, because Taleb has a number of endearing qualities. I just felt disappointed that we hadn't been able to bring the best out of him. He played some startlingly good matches, including some of the best squash of the tour. Once, in Bangkok, he played the best of three sets with Jawaid and beat him 2–0, providing a revelation of how to play the game as far as technique and tactics were concerned. If I were to write an article on the game, I think I would write on Taleb *v.* Jawaid in Bangkok. It was absolutely superb.

He saved the show on more than one occasion. When the crowd were becoming a little bored I would send him on and take the refereeing job myself. He would then go through his enormous repertoire of tricks and I would deliver him a few public warnings as to future conduct on the court, producing incredible roars of delight from the crowds. Taleb would apologise to me: 'Sorry, sir', and that sort of thing and I'd say: 'If there's any more of this. . . .' What a performance! Abou sees things very simply and was very loyal to me during the tour. He acts instinctively, like a trapped bear; it seems sometimes as if he's caught and has found himself surrounded by an awful lot of things he can't comprehend. He can't understand why other players have excelled him, although he is perhaps beginning to realise that it is because there has been such a tremendous advance in physical fitness and that players are less afraid of his type of game than they were seven years ago.

I was sore of course when he failed to show up for the P.I.A. evening and the Benson and Hedges series, because I had paid the fare for him to see his wife in Cairo. I *think* the main reason why he didn't turn up was that he had heard he was seeded No 8 in the British Open—which was a disgrace.

I was seeded 1, Jawaid 2 and Yasin 3. Taleb should have been No 4, and certainly neither Rainer nor Sharif would have quibbled. In championship play they had not beaten him and you do not judge a man's standard from a series of exhibition matches. You judge a man's standard on what he does in major competition when the chips are down and the pressure on.

The British Open meant big business for me as my contract with Dunlop was drawing to a close. I had won the Australian Championship to get back the No 1 spot and had to clinch this without the Australians present. So I had to work and attune my mind to this with all consideration for the other players set aside.

By the time the British Open started, I felt that I had brought myself to a peak I had never reached before. I had climbed a personal Everest. I didn't have Hunt playing against me and I thought that whoever came on court against me was merely there to be chopped down. I played the best squash of my life without any shadow of doubt. I was decisive and unmerciful; very accurate and offered no hospitality when out of hand. I got the service back through disciplined play and then was most positive. I displayed a much wider variety of kill strokes than ever before in a major championship and I think it pleased the press to see me play spectacular and yet percentage squash—what might be spectacular for somebody else was becoming percentage for me. A cross-court nick overhead was actually in the chart now.

For the final I was, to say the least, in a very severe and determined mood. I was absolutely determined to get it out of Aftab's mind that he was a better player than me. I had helped him in Pakistan, yet out there he had given the impression that I had actually asked him if he would allow me to win. His suggestion had been that I had to win to be seen in a good light, but that I couldn't win if he didn't want me to. I was determined to put the record straight.

In practice, when I was playing without any thought or concentration, Jawaid would beat me because he was like a robot. Whether he played matches or practice he still played the same way. If a player wasn't concentrating against him then he had no chance whether he was Hunt, Barrington or anyone else.

But when I was concentrating and disciplined there was no way in which Aftab could beat me. I was fitter than him; I was as patient and I had many more positive strokes. This proved to be so, because in that 1970 British Open final he collected only 9 points. In fact, he shouldn't have reached six in the third game, but I got a bit of elbow and produced a couple of unforced errors when out of hand, which was unforgivable. My game had come to the boil at the right time to a greater extent than had occurred since December 1966 when I suddenly played points above my previous best to beat Corby, Taleb, Amin and Jawaid in successive rounds. I felt in practice on my own that the ball was going to go just where I wanted it to go; my reactions were razor-sharp. It was a great feeling and I wanted to retain it for ever and ever. It was something akin to complete satisfaction within a certain sphere.

The British Open ended and now we were on the final lap, the Benson and Hedges round-robin.

This was a success because no one had done it before and where the venue was properly promoted the gallery was over-subscribed, which was what we wanted. There were one or two disasters but generally things went well. At Bournemouth they were hanging from the rafters. I was undefeated in the series though a number of matches went to five and I was match point down to Jawaid one evening. Yasin came through to beat Jawaid twice in what was, for Aftab, a trying time. He was beaten in the Amateur Championships very surprisingly by Billy Reedman whom I would expect to beat him not more than once in 50 matches. This was very rough on Aftab, who obviously had a chance of winning the British Amateur again, particularly when John Easter took Nancarrow in the other half.

Yasin seemed to get over his psychological fear of Aftab on this tour and looked likely to go on to greater things. But he then decided not to play any more competitions outside our series on the pretext that he was injured. Perhaps he really did have a bad leg although this was difficult to appreciate while he was playing in our round-robin since he performed admirably against Sharif and Rainer in the last two matches of the tour to clinch the No 2 spot.

But he always seemed to have trouble whenever a tournament loomed up. Both at Sutton and St Anne's he was drawn to play Alauddin, the young Pakistani, who had just won the Amateur Championship and was going particularly well. He withdrew, however, from the confrontation and this lack of positive thinking leads me to believe that Yasin will never take the major titles. He is slightly negative in his approach and has a fear of so many things that he will never really climb right to the top.

Within the group accord was dwindling even more. There was the Pakistani faction of Jawaid and Yasin who spent most of their time talking in Urdu, much to the annoyance of Rainer. Alauddin played in a couple of extra matches and when there were three of them talking in the language it was almost impossible. I kept away as much as possible and put the brunt of the management on to Rainer who did in fact do the driving in the Benson and Hedges car. Sharif was admirably loyal and backed me in every possible way, which marks him with a far better stamp than the others. But for Rainer and Sharif at that time the tour would have foundered because, without a doubt, Aftab was playing the role of Mephistopheles and playing it pretty well.

The tour was completed very successfully at the Lansdowne Club on January 24. The players broke up, much to my relief, and the tour had come to an end. When one thinks that we started on about August 15 and went through nearly to the end of January it is easy to see what a monumental promotion it was. My views on it can be put fairly concisely.

I felt that it was impossible to put on further tours of that nature because financially it didn't pay a big enough dividend. The gates were not, could not, be large enough and unless you had a formidable sponsorship you couldn't even cover your costs. There is no way one can put on a tour on traditional courts as a financial proposition.

Neither did I want to put on another tour with top players, because I felt that they had behaved like a lot of prima-donnas. It is difficult for a player who is directly involved at the top and striving to retain his position to manage another group of players who are constantly trying to knock him off. If I was No 2, No 3 or No 4 player, I would not like to be ordered around by a person who was there just above me.

As I grow older and the top players perhaps become younger there will come a time when I will feel quite confident to control a group, to drive them and administer a programme without much friction.

I can foresee more circuses of players, though not perhaps for three to five years unless the right sponsor comes along or unless we have a see-through court. Until then any tours will be conducted with two or three players at maximum. The five-man or the eight-man group will have to wait until the facilities are better both for spectators and TV.

In the middle of the Benson and Hedges series we played a tournament at St Anne's which provided a confrontation between Barrington and Nancarrow, the first for a couple of years. I managed to dislodge him 9–7, 9–7, 9–0, the last game an extremely satisfactory one which endeared me to myself for a long time afterwards. The first two games were very tough and could have gone either way. Both of us had trouble in playing freely against each other but it was a furious battle mentally.

At this time I had certain personal problems which attracted substantial publicity in national newspapers. Three press hounds were snooping at Cheltenham when the circus played there but with the connivance of Geoff Davis, the club proprietor, and the aid of a diversion created by Sharif who pretended to want to sell them his life story, a clean getaway was effected via the changing-room window. Inevitably it was only a temporary relief for next day fifteen pressmen were hanging around outside Clive Francis's house in St Anne's waiting to interview me. I decided that I wasn't going to say a word about anything—not even 'NO COMMENT'—but the pressure was extreme. In the end, the club wouldn't allow the press into the club except on the semi-final night. They were determined to take photographs and I agreed that they could if they were taken on the court—because I was a squash player. If they wanted photographs they could have photographs of a squash player and not a lover walking down the promenade at Blackpool.

So the press came on. Six in all. Two by two they came and I did my best to make their lives unpleasant as I unrelentingly fired vicious salvos to the left and right of them. Cam Nancarrow obligingly fed the balls to me and thought this was most amusing. In the end the gallery started applauding. I was grateful because I was just there to play squash, whereas these people were determined to interfere in my private life—it was nothing to do with them.

As far as I was concerned, my private life is my private life. You can't detach sport from politics and you can't wholly detach the public figure from what goes on in his private life; but there is a certain area of his private life which should not be invaded. This the press refuse to acknowledge and they behaved in a preposterous fashion. The only thing about the situation which pleased me was that instead of faltering under the pressure I became even more determined to murder the opposition. I went through the tournament without dropping a set and this time poor Aftab, in the final, got only 8 points.

After the Benson and Hedges series there was the Cutty Sark Tournament at Sutton where I played Nancarrow in the final. I was starting to go off the boil and had a very rugged match with him that went on for about an hour and twenty-five minutes. I beat him in five games after being two games down and 0–5 in the third. I finally came through only with an enormous amount of self-control, having been forced into a battle down the backhand wall in which he was completely out-playing me. It only remained for me to hit the last four balls into the tin as I had done on a couple of previous occasions, but I managed to gather myself together and get on top. From the moment I got the third game I knew that, providing I kept my head, there was little doubt that I would win because he was getting so tired.

The pressure was off. I tried to get myself organised, to settle down and to find a little peace and quiet. I played one or two exhibitions with Rainer and my final competition of the season was at Stockton in the middle of February where I beat Taleb 3–0 in the final, Taleb having taken out Rainer in the semi-final.

On that match hangs a tale. Rainer had over-subscribed his views to *Squash Rackets News* on the subject of Taleb, saying that we had carried him on tour and that he was a bit of a joke. So much so that Taleb came out in a bellicose mood for their battle and played a superb match to win in five. Rainer was unable to sit down or get up the following day. I was then committed to a five-week tour with Clive Francis, the British Professional Champion, the professional at St Anne's and an assiduous worker of the Northern circuit.

We played about 30 exhibitions, often two on one night, gave about 15 clinics and tried to spread the gospel around the North. It was a hard tour but not as hard as the one that had gone before. I felt a little bit lack-lustre and what I really wanted was to get away from having to think and talk about the game, and get quietly stuck into my training. But it was a most interesting experiment and I think it did have a good effect in that part of the world.

My personal problems hit an even worse pitch at this stage and I was soon on my own again. I wanted just to get away—anywhere. As it happened an invitation came to go to Canada for 18 days so I went to Toronto to play some exhibitions with Sharif and give some clinics. I went on April 10th not in the best of humour and feeling very run down even though I'd still been doing my training.

You're either on the boil, or you're off the boil. Barrington was off the boil. When I got to Canada I was terrifically well received at Ralph Gardiner's Skyline Club in Toronto and was really made to feel welcome. I played my first exhibition match on those very peculiar American courts with Sharif and

Kenny Binns the Australian pro I had last played in Newcastle, New South Wales, on my first tour and had then beaten 9–7 in the fifth. I took both of them and played pretty well so I had a successful start to my tour. Sharif and I were sparring amicably off the court as well as on: Barrington was clad in a blue velvet suit which caused a great stir and things didn't seem too bad after all. I felt that I was going to kick myself out of my lethargy.

This was not to be, because, two days later, I got a stomach infection and in 8 days lost 9 lbs. Those 8 days I spent most of my time disappearing in and out of the bathroom. I had to give clinics and exhibitions, which were very lucrative, but unfortunately during all this I constantly had to nip on and off court. I felt very, very, weak, very unwell and never recovered the weight until the middle of the summer of 1971.

This was an unbelievable shock to the system. I must have had some form of dysentery but it was a damn sight worse than any other stomach disorder that I've had. Sharif was beating me in the exhibitions, although he let me win two or three and could have won the others much more easily than he did. I was very, very depressed and when I came back at the end of the month, the day before my birthday, I had the overnight journey from Canada. This involves the time change so you miss your sleep completely. You arrive at 3.00 a.m. Toronto time but it's 8.30 a.m. in London. Just when you feel like going to bed you've got to wake up because it's daylight and breakfast. That evening I flew off to Greece for the Greek Open Championship. I then didn't get to bed till about 4 or 5 in the morning so, on top of the infection that I'd had, I hadn't in fact slept for 48 hours.

If ever Barrington was run down it was then. I tried to produce best endeavours as always but reckon that probably 100 squash players in the world could have beaten me. As it happened I lost to two Egyptians Kaoud (in an invitation) and Asran (in the Greek Open). All that can be said was that on the day these boys played very well. I fought like a dog, as is my wont, but there was nothing there. They were better than me on that day. Although I could expect to beat them 99 times out of a 100, the lesson had to be learned: don't go playing in competition, exposing yourself, when you are not fully prepared. If you have time changes, ensure that you have a long break before playing a serious match. These are hard lessons and at the age of 30 you still go on learning. A top player is there to be shot at and he can't afford to be ill-prepared for a battle.

I went to Greece with a fine group of characters who don't purport to be world champions but they are at the same time the sort of people who make the game what it is. Amongst them there were a couple of younger players who were training as hard as any young players have ever trained in Britain for squash. Our tour was sponsored by Rent-a-Villa; with whose Rent-a-Villa track-suits we disarmed the natives of the Greek island of Poros, as we marched through in our cavalcade. We did court training on the roof of a villa, much to the amazement of the local residents. It was quite an experience but I was in a shocking state when I returned to London to take up a contract with the Squash Rackets Association: for ten weeks I was to train the British team—Corby, Easter, Ayton and Millman—which was to challenge for the world team title in New Zealand.

The flat I was provided with was totally unsatisfactory and I settled into the Lansdowne Club where I started to work out with Naz's two sons, Rehmat and Aman, and move into my own training schedule.

The first week was disastrous. I lost to every member of the British team and was almost at the point or packing the whole contract in. I then managed to pick myself off the ground and thereafter lost only one match. I played two players a night and on one night Philip Ayton, second on, beat me.

I feel that the training was to a very great extent ineffective. This was not the fault of the manager, Peter Chalk, but perhaps more my fault in that it is very difficult to assert authority over players of one's own generation.

It wasn't a team training in the true sense of the term. If a team is training, it trains together, because the most vital part is the team spirit that is engendered over a long period. Working together, getting to know each other really well and building up a team spirit will not necessarily take a team to the title, but it will show up well on a tour and act as a stepping stone for the future. I don't think anybody else could have handled the team better than the manager Peter Chalk, but at the same time the players were loath to work together. Paul Millman may have trained on his own but he did no training with anybody else except for playing on the three official practice nights. Training schedules take place over a whole week. One or two players wanted a rest period but I felt that schedules should be for much longer than ten weeks, and that if necessary the team should not have been chosen till a month before they went away. If there is any suspicion of a weakness in a man's character, it's certainly much more difficult to bring out the best in him when he knows regardless of effort that he's still going to travel. I think the players work much harder when they are still in doubt. They grumble, they think that it is unfair pressure, but surely that's what it's all about. World-class sport is pressure.

The training started too late and was not very satisfactory. I played two players a night throughout the training which was obviously necessary, but there should have been much more besides. There was some running but nothing that could compare with the training the England Badminton squad did at R.A.F. Innsworth under Bomber Harris. My squad would not survive more than one session of that. The games are in some ways similar. Both are tremendously arduous, require tremendous stamina, and the ability to recover from a vicious rally very quickly without making errors.

I very much hope that, in future, we will get away from the old-established idea that the team can put in a superficial ten-week programme and also that a squad of 8 or even 10 players, previously regarded as unwieldy, will be chosen. That squad can then be whittled down to the four who will travel through a competitive round-robin condensed into little more than a week. It will only be necessary to do this about three or four weeks beforehand, so a large squad will be working and retaining the animal's primitive instinct for survival to the last.

My worst fear was that Britain would come fourth. In fact, they were second, which one could say was the best position they could have hoped for. At the same time, I felt they should have beaten the U.A.R. 2–1 instead of losing 2–1 and that they should have come a clear second though many lengths behind Australia as they were in 1969 and 1967. There is obviously some talent and potential there which, if integrated with other younger talent that is already showing itself, might produce the right attitude and approach for the next world title in 1973.

I was quite certain that no player in the British team could win the individual title. The best we could hope for was to get a quarter-finalist. In fact, we had two quarter-finalists, which was a very reasonable effort. John Easter made a big advance over the previous 12 months and should continue to do so if he is prepared to put the work in. He is a big man and must keep in condition. He can't afford to take a month or two off and then come back as some of the other players do. He is a very determined, very gutsy performer. During the ten weeks of team training he did an immense amount of work and reduced himself again and again. This produced a severe reaction on the court at times, but though he became pretty depressed and miserable, he still fought his way through.

Philip Ayton is a very intelligent player with a strange but effective style. If anything he's a little bit too much of a loner and I don't know that he really appreciates taking advice. I think it is a fatal flaw in anyone not to draw the strength out of other people in this way. Philip prefers to do all the work himself and not rely on anybody else, whereas my success sprang from Nasrullah and Azam Khan. What they taught me I can teach other people if they are prepared to listen.

Mike Corby is one of the most interesting sportsmen in Britain. As time goes by, one sees more and more robots, manufactured talents, puppets on strings. Mike Corby does not follow any established creed except his own, and this changes from day to day. He's immensely likable yet, like most erratic individuals, can be intensely infuriating. A lot of people might say this of me. I think Mike's basic lack of discipline and a degree of self-delusion have prevented him reaching the heights in squash. We have always had good matches but he has not beaten me for six years. Though Mike has lost immensely well on many occasions to world-class players, the mark of a man is what he wins, not how well he loses. Had he not talked his way into thinking he was a first-class player and talked his way out of defeats, I think that he would have been a far greater player. But as a celebrated hockey international also, he remains one of Britain's most exciting sportsmen.

11

Reflections—1972

Jonah Barrington

Squash was held in a state of stagnation in Britain for a very long time. During the last five years we have been forcing the issue and there are now healthy signs of progress. The snowballing effect will be continued because there's nothing that anybody can now do to prevent it, and I say 'to prevent it', because undoubtedly in 1964 there were those within the S.R.A. administration who preferred to see a narrow, public school set-up, the old school tie network, regardless of whether the British game remained in a decomposed state with total lack of success against the best overseas opposition. So-called show-piece matches were really just a good opportunity to get together and have an almighty, great booze-up with the squash as an unfortunate adjunct.

The classic example of this has been the Strawson Memorial match which is supposed to open the British season in October. I will always remember in 1966 a comment before the Strawson that 'strangely' a lot of players would be fit. This was considered to be quite extraordinary and not quite right—an approach that infuriates me and is only too typical of the diseased vegetable which constituted the S.R.A. throughout the 50's and early 60's.

In Britain, squash is moving on from being just an upper-class game in public schools, universities and the forces and now is becoming rather more like Badminton. Squash has changed completely in that players are realising that they have to work at the game both on and off the court to reach any standard at all. When I started, in 64/65, you were considered completely abnormal if you went on the court after the middle of April, because the summer had begun and it was too hot for squash. This traditional argument has gone completely by the board and it is now realised that, to have any success at all, one needs to work for eleven months each year at least.

With the growth of facilities in Britain, more and more clubs are allowing kids to come in off-peak hours and adult participants are now coming from a wider section of society, which will be all to the good.

I have tried to change the assumption that the Pakistani, the Australian or the Arab has that much greater flair for playing our sport than we do. I have tried to apply myself as I would expect top competitors to apply themselves. The great examples of this, of course, are the top Australian sportsmen who take their responsibilities seriously, make the necessary sacrifices to reach the top, and then continue to do so to retain that position.

I wanted to change the Establishment's attitude to professionals: that the professional was not quite satisfactory because he tended to sully himself by taking money, prostituting his talent for the game. The general impression was that the professional was merely a dog to whom the bone would be thrown at the end of the meal; he couldn't be allowed to eat the meal with everyone else on the same level. It was a class-conscious situation which had to go and we have already travelled some distance in the right direction. It has also been part of my plan to campaign for Open squash. I think everyone will benefit from this. Both I and other professional players would obviously be able to play many more tournaments and this would make it that much easier to keep a competitive edge. Open squash will allow far more people to take what is still considered rather a gamble. Financially, it will be a good move to turn professional, to be a full-time player, whereas now a man's enthusiasm for doing so has been tempered because this move has tended to end his competitive career. With one or two exceptions it has been a barren field; nothing has happened, nothing has been sown and nothing has been reaped.

We must have masters to teach pupils, and I don't feel the real teachers will come from the ranks of the qualified amateur coaches. Although these men have provided a very necessary interim service, we want real professionals and we will have these with the advent of Open squash.

The world scene has changed a great deal since I came into the game. Squash has gained a hold in more countries, notably Sweden. Japan will be the sensation of the seventies. The international game is developing: there's a World Amateur Championship; there's a swing towards Open squash which may or may not happen for a couple of years.

The Americans have no chance of projecting their game and their courts further afield because, from every point of view, our game is better than theirs. We have an international ball whereas theirs is confined to North America and possibly Mexico. I don't ever see the two games drawing together because their smaller courts just aren't satisfactory with our ball. What I do see is that their game will still survive, as Eton Fives and Rackets have survived here, but that our game will go into North America with our specifications. This may involve some internal turmoil for the American S.R.A., but I see no other way.

My contribution to the development of the game has been, I believe, a tremendous emphasis on fitness and correct preparation. When I first won the Open, I was way behind the champions of the past, although I had a basic game that was sensible and practical. The crux of the matter was that my opponents all felt that I was far fitter than them. Geoff Hunt's contribution is far greater technically because I have copied him. He was the innovator, in the late 60's, of the volleying technique round the middle of the court, pressure volleys to the back of the court, the deep length game. Jawaid had shown this to a lesser degree, without the volley, in the middle or early 60's. By taking the ball much earlier than Jawaid, Geoff put the ball in the same place as him but half a second earlier.

Taleb found that by the middle of the 60's he couldn't win a major championship, though in the early 60's he had been able

John Easter. A very promising young English International whose height gives him a prodigious reach. Once a male model, he was described by Rex Bellamy of *The Times* as the 'Matinée Idol'.

Jonah in action in Sheffield. Always superbly fit, he is able to make the most of his speed and reach even at the end of a long game.

Ken Hiscoe (Australia) whose intelligent play had seriously threatened Jonah's game in the 1967 Amateur semi-finals. He remains a superb technical exponent of the game.

'Dedication.'

Jonah in the ‘ready’ position.

The ‘crab’—a study in movement.

to win them with some ease. I think what we have learned in the last six or seven years is that unless you are especially fit you can't win one of the major championships of the world. Regardless of how superb your technique is, if you can't reach the ball, you can't hit it. Geoff's technique has been copied widely: taking the ball earlier, cutting off, not giving way; when you're tired having a bit of a breather, slowballing, then, when you've got your breath back, putting in another fiery burst. This is a superb technique which won him the 1967 World Amateur Championship. In his semi-final against Ken Hiscoe, he won the first two games, but Ken came back to win the third 9–0 and was 7–0 up in the fourth. He then eased off for a couple of points and Geoff put in one of those incredible bursts of power play, fast hitting, fast movement in the middle of the court to take the match and reach the final.

The most important thing to me, in squash, is winning at the highest level. There are a number of other things I want to do. I want to make money out of the game; I want to build a business; produce my own players; have my own squad and train by own world champions of the future. But for the moment, I want to be World Champion and remain so for a long time. I am only too aware of the driving force in my life because when I play badly I am so miserable about it that I can barely contain myself. Squash is not the be all and end all of my life but I don't need the sort of diversions that a lot of people have. To me it's very pleasant to have a quiet evening watching television. I don't want to go to parties.

What I do find now is that I'm more prepared to rest than I was before. I'll rest up, arrange my time more skilfully and won't confine myself to the squash court for the whole day. Equally, when a man has reached the age of 30 and has travelled all over the world, constantly on the move, he wearies of it and its limitations.

Until 1970 I felt I was not strong enough to give less than 100% of my mental and physical energies to squash. I can use people but I tread warily with emotions—my own as well as theirs. My self-discipline as far as women were concerned was part of a consuming self-discipline. I was so much aware that my squash had been manufactured and that younger players were improving, that I could not let go for a moment. I could not afford the tiniest chink in my armour.

But a man grows tired of wandering all over the place; this gradually gnaws at him but is accepted provided there is no alternative. If there does come an alternative, if he does fall in love or something equally devastating, then, wherever he goes, he will constantly think: 'I'd like to have a base and be more settled; I'd like to be looked after and look after somebody, to take more responsibilities, to have a family.' This would be easy enough providing there were no complications. In my own case, I fell in love with someone who is already married so there are a thousand other complications.

My sport is consuming but it is not as consuming as it was. It was once all-consuming because I didn't want to do anything else, whereas now I want and have other things to do. I also know more and therefore get through enough work in a shorter time to allow me to perhaps watch television or write a letter. I used to be stiff with tension because my whole day was spent in thinking about a ball and racket. I went to bed at night and my thoughts turned to squash. It was obvious that a change would have to come but not that it would come in the way it did. As one matures, so one wants to become involved with other things. One is still travelling down the same track but at the same time one wants to branch out and deal with other things. It's great to have something really on the move but then one starts looking for other areas of interest. As far as I'm concerned, the greatest area of interest for a man, once he's determined his career, which I have, is to have a wife and family, because that is something that will travel with him, an aspect of his life which he can in a sense put on automatic pilot after a while and concentrate on other things.

At the start of my career Nasrullah demanded discipline. Without this I might have found myself involved in more casual affairs but, firstly, one can't be certain that a casual affair won't become a very serious affair and, secondly, people who are sensitive don't particularly want to take another person for a ride. Anything I do, I do with serious intent. If I fall in love, I fall in love very seriously. I don't dilly-dally. Anyone who has played up any relationship of mine as a chance affair has made a serious error.

A top sportsman is regarded as a challenge by some women. I have had a lot of opportunities and no doubt there will be a lot of opportunities in the future. But what is it all about? In the sport I play, the foundation of the game is discipline but that discipline has to overflow outside the squash court, particularly in things that directly relate to the game. To be fresh when I go on court I must eat well, sleep well, and lead an organised, disciplined life. There will be those who will laugh at this, remembering that I am generally at least half an hour late for any appointment; this is a weakness, a lack of discipline, the Achilles heel in my armoury of discipline, I suppose. But I never arrive late for my match, when I can be scratched ten minutes after the appointed time.

Squash doesn't give complete happiness: it never will. It provides one, if successful, with a fickle popularity, a certain amount of glory, which is always pleasing to the ego, and more money and comforts than before; for these I am grateful. I must not and will not let this go, so I have got to work a delicate balance between this and other parts of my life.

There is a rich satisfaction when the work one has put in, the practice, the training one has endured, brings the reward of a major championship and the delight of a good win over a challenger. This is a fleeting satisfaction but the moment does provide pleasure. Happiness has many facets to it and the whole may well be unattainable.

12

In the Teeth of Adversity

Clive Everton

While the British team laboured in New Zealand, Jonah put himself out to pasture. He had travelled a good deal the previous year and for the time being he didn't want to travel any more.

Peter Webb, the most enthusiastic squash player in England, lent Jonah a flat above one of his hairdressing shops in Solihull and the pressure was relaxed at last. At the West Warwickshire Club he ran round the cricket field and played tennis furiously with Johnny Prescott, the former heavyweight boxer, but squash he played hardly at all. It was a fallow period.

For the first time since I had known him, it appeared that he was beginning to learn how to relax, necessarily so since the relentless travelling of 1970, culminating in sorties to Canada (where he had dysentery) and Greece, whence he had travelled without proper rest, had led to his system becoming so run down that his return to England brought an outbreak of boils in his ears, eight in one, three in the other.

As September passed into October and then into November, Jonah visibly gathered momentum. He was starting to talk of the Open and it was clear that he was now starting to channel his thoughts and energies single-mindedly in this direction. He gave a few clinics and played a few exhibitions but Jonah is not a man to put himself out in pursuit of money. He would rather spend money training than earn money coaching and his fees for exhibitions and clinics were kept at a level which, though by no means unrealistic, surprisingly appeared to discourage all but the keenest.

While the money in this fallow time would not have been surplus to requirements, it is simply not Jonah's nature to relate his style of living or the money he spends to current income, particularly in view of the fact that he undertook for some six months the entire expense of looking after Amanullah Khan, Nazrullah's elder son and disbursed certain personal loans, few if any of which were repaid.

His contracts provided the income for him to live comfortably, though not indefinitely off them, but when Hunt and Hiscoe turned professional and showed no inclination to include Jonah in their plans, as Jonah had included Hunt in his, the possibility of (and to a great extent the desire for) a Kramer-like troupe of players receded.

Jonah liked the idea of a touring troupe in the sense of creating something which had not existed before but he was deeply opposed to drawing any kind of return from another player's efforts. This fine feeling was not shared by other players, who fed off him like locusts. Jonah's natural generosity with money and hospitality particularly in the purchasing of meals in restaurants (whenever Jonah was about to eat, hordes of players would be magically in attendance) was relentlessly exploited to a point where it finally occurred to him that a Barrington troupe would never be regarded a common enterprise but merely as a way of living comfortably off Barrington. When he had his headquarters at the Lansdowne, not a lunchtime would pass without someone calling to see him—with a business idea, to ask a favour, or simply for a chat. One common factor was that it cost Jonah money. A champion is regarded as a form of public property: people write for training schedules and pictures, issue invitations to dinners and dances and require an incredible variety of favours. Business schemes proliferate.

Almost all of them offer 'enormous potential', wealth beyond the dreams of avarice when sales top a certain figure but alas no guarantee of *any* sales or so low a guarantee that its contrast with the limitless aspiration of the 'enormous potential' is bound to sound a cautionary note. Chains of Jonah Barrington Squash Centres are discussed but the question that is asked is how much money Jonah is prepared to put in rather than the question we wish to ask: how much does Jonah take out?

We managed to insulate Jonah from some of the grosser attempts to waste his time but some slipped through. There again, some of the offers are worth pursuing and do eventually yield a return though heavily outnumbered by attempts to exploit his name or reputation without remuneration.

Jonah is essentially a free-booting buccaneer in spirit. It is a pity squash had not reached the stage of tennis's development with all-year-round big tournaments for big prize money. Such a world, where income is related very directly to results, is one to which his philosophy of life is sympathetic. But in squash, as yet, prize money, taken annually, is insignificant compared with contracts which are negotiated—in the scheming world of business in airless boardrooms or over heavy lunches—rather than won, in open public view, through man to man combat. It was a situation to which Jonah, in his boundless ambition, frequently reacted with bitter frustration, though frustration is perhaps, in the nature of things, an inevitable companion for life's overreachers.

But on the surface all seemed well as he ploughed on with his training until December 6th, seven weeks from the Open, he was stricken by influenza. Five days later, he could still not rise from his bed and was now unable to eat because of his ulcerated mouth and swollen gums. His mouth was infected, certain glands were permanently swollen and he had two impacted wisdom teeth. Look at it how one might, he was in a bad way.

His meticulous training schedule was shattered and though the medical profession effected a temporary and partial recovery desperate measures were clearly called for. On Boxing Day, he and Aman took a plane to Nairobi to train at altitude.

Jonah: 'Kenya has many obvious advantages. It is a country warm by nature and full of delightful surprises. I was met by a consuming kindness which opened all doors and which gently drew me away from this pervading pressure building up at home. The schedule was clinically simply. In the morning, up to an hour's intensive running and another hour of practising on my own on the court; in the late afternoon another practice, perhaps for thirty minutes, a long game played on handicap with Aman, and some court training to finish. This four-hour schedule bore no fruit initially but the work was being put in. However, by the 10th of January, my mouth had become infected again. I had to cast aside all events bar the British Open—there had to be just the one monumental effort.'

This involved Jonah's disengagement from two tournaments conveying substantial prize money, the Cutty Sark and the Grandee Series. I felt more like an unagent than an agent, tidying up the ends and fending off multitudinous requests for information. A lady who had clearly been squash correspondent for a respected provincial paper for many years was one who enquired Jonah's whereabouts.

'He's in Kenya.'

'What's he doing there?'

'Altitude training.'

'Oh, jumping out of aeroplanes and free falling. What fun.'

'No, it's not quite like that. The theory is that if one runs and trains under pressure well above sea level, performance will be easier and therefore improved when one returns to sea level.'

'But how is this relevant to squash?'

It was a wearing time.

Jonah: 'I knew the many vultures were out at home, awaiting my demise, and this spurred me to a greater work rate. In those last two weeks I trained more efficiently and with greater zest than at any time during the last seven years. I was going to be a wee bit rusty but bloody hard to beat.

That one or two silly men were trying change the rules of the game, without even having the decency to consult its leading players again hardened the killer resolve within me. Why do officials always legislate against the players? We can so often sort out our own problems, especially as the current generation of squash players tend to be fair on the court—unlike so many ill-mannered and physically intimidating "good" British players in the 50's. Ken Hiscoe put it quite succinctly recently with his comment that the administration here "was a lot of bloody little messes"—I like that appraisal!'

The S.R.A. directive, subsequently revoked after an almost unanimous howl of protest, sought to penalise players who stamped as they hit the ball or bounced it before serving. Jonah's own appraisal of what many (including his chief opponents) interpreted as measures directed chiefly against him appeared in *The Squash Player*.

On January 28th, Jonah reached Sheffield for the tournament, his path smoothed by the withdrawals of Sharif Khan and Yasin from his section. He won two easy rounds, feeling good and looking good, and was then stricken by a stomach infection which caused him to divide his time between bed and toilet with only two visits to the squash court to play Ray Lewis in the last 16 and Gallal Allam in the last 8. Neither appreciated to the full how Jonah was feeling though the press commented that he had gone ultradefensive.

Jonah: 'My oath! So would the press if they were suffering from the dissolution of their intestines as I was. I felt a little better by the time I played Alauddin—if I hadn't felt a little better I would have scratched—but I still did not have the resources or the edge to win positively. The press described it as a dull match and I was content to win dully in three games.'

13

The Open Final

Dicky Rutnagur

(*The Squash Player*, March 1972)

A deep reservoir of energy, a highly sophisticated sense of tactics and an indomitable spirit saw Jonah Barrington through another cruel marathon with his old rival, Geoff Hunt, in the final of the Benson & Hedges British Open Championship.

The final margin was slight—9–7, the scores in the first four games being (Barrington first) 0–9, 9–7, 10–8, 6–9. Battle raged for 115 minutes.

Barrington has now won the British Open often enough to earn him an honorary membership of the Khan clan. It was his third triumph in a row and his fifth in six years. Only Hashim Khan's name appears more often—seven times—on the roll of honour.

After the last 16 stage of the tournament, the final was the only match of which the outcome was in the balance. Its dramatic impact was augmented by the weight of the winner's purse (£500) and, even more, by the atmosphere of the new championship court at the Abbeydale Park Squash Club, Sheffield.

The glass back wall and the low standing galleries on the side gave the spectators a closer and improved view of the proceedings. The players, in turn, must have felt an enhanced sense of gallery participation in their elation, their disappointments and their fatigue.

Jonah: 'As a playing surface the new glass back wall was almost completely satisfactory. Any problems of adjusting to it were so minimal that they were dominated by the fact that it produced a far more exciting atmosphere and a much more cosmopolitan crowd than the tiny coterie which invariably witness the Lansdowne or Edgbaston Priory finals.

The mind is so concentrated on the ball that one is conscious of the spectators only after the rally is over although it was noticeable that Jawaid, who has always swung most freely out of the corners, was not so much at ease.

The court provided the first real link with a realistic competitive future. Not a great many championship courts of this size will be built although glass back walls will certainly be used in many new centres.'

As the two track-suited figures of Barrington and Hunt came through the wings at the side of the court, laid down their burden of spare rackets, extra shirts and jumbo-sized towels near the sight boards and then gingerly unlatched the glass door to take the court, the crowd experienced the thrill of being present at a truly big and important sporting event.

Barrington, with the good grace of the perfect host, held the door open for Hunt to stride in first. As Barrington snapped the latch back, the crowd burst into thunderous applause which drowned the sounds of the first few shots of the knock-up.

Barrington bases every important and difficult campaign on the strategy of playing a long first game. But on this occasion, he could not stretch the initial engagement beyond 15 minutes and, what is more, had the rare experience of being beaten at love. Rallies were long, but never intensely fierce and Hunt came out of the game fresher than his opponent would have wanted.

Jonah: 'And with no chink in his armour. I had exposed nothing, save the fact that I was very short of this quality of match play. I had a little discussion with Nasrullah at the end of that first game, sorting out the basic tactic, the lob to his backhand high. If it wasn't played well, he would destroy it but I wasn't equipped at that time to take set offensive so attrition was the only course open.'

Only eight hands were played in this game and Geoff had two runs of four points each. Considering the easy pace, Barrington's error rate was high and his responses to drop shots were also slow. Clearly, he looked gripped by the tension.

Jonah: 'My error rate perhaps was high, though many of them were forced, but he was error free and playing to a very tight pattern whereas I was still stiff from playing Gogi in the semi-final. I can be *quite* sharp with no match practice but in one or two areas—like playing Hunt—one cannot, on the practice court, simulate the real thing.

Anyone who had seen my sharpness in the last British Open would realise that that edge was missing. After all the training I had done I was very fit. I could have beaten anyone in the tournament over twenty-three miles and I knew I could play for a long time. But at what pace? That was the question.'

Geoff continued to make almost unhampered progress till 4–0 in the second game. Once more, these four points had been claimed in one hand. At this stage, service changed hands five times without either player gaining ground. Barrington eventually scraped up his first point from a misaimed back-hand volley by Hunt. A forehand drive gave Jonah the second winner he had struck so far, in almost half an hour, the first having been at the fag end of the first game.

Jonah: 'Geoff was still doing everything perfectly but the rallies were becoming longer. He couldn't kill as quickly and I was making less errors. Mentally, I was starting to ease and, conversely, he felt a little tension creeping in. Having won the first game easily, he may well have thought that I was now starting to come back as I had in the past. He felt his first tiredness in the middle of this second game. In fact, unlike any other player, he tires again and again and still comes back.'

There were three lets for the next point and, getting restive,

Geoff again hit the tin. This made it 3–4 to Barrington, who proceeded to get even with a hefty forehand volley.

A deep shot by Hunt on Barrington's backhand got him his service back and another good length took him to 5. Barrington almost duplicated this shot to get in again, only to fail on a forcing backhand volley.

Then there was a rare penalty point given against Geoff. Back in hand, Jonah played a screaming forehand winner along the wall. Detecting a slight relief of pressure, he assumed a more aggressive attitude and got up to 8–5.

Hunt gave Barrington's next service the charge and killed it. Twice Barrington was in hand at 8–6, and both times Hunt gained a reprieve with rousing winners. But when he served for the game a fourth time, at 8–7, Barrington broke down on a backhand drive. The fifth time, also at 8–7, he deprived himself by missing a backhand drop.

It must be said to Hunt's credit that even when hand out, he attempted the most daring shots. He finally came unstuck against a lovely, lobbed service which he just failed to get back.

Jonah: 'Is any service that good against a top class player? The fact was that Hunt will go so far and then crack. When he does crack, he makes hideous mistakes and this was one of them.'

This vital second game lasted only a minute under half an hour and the third too was of the same duration, although half as many hands were played.

Barrington started hesitantly and Hunt ruthlessly accumulated a 6–1 lead, which he dissipated quite swiftly. Put out by a backhand volley drop, he hit the tin four times running and then put a lob out of court. This made it 6–all. There was now a long, breath-taking rally during which both players attacked and retrieved with desperate fury.

This was probably the most spectacular rally of the match. Ironically, it was brought to a halt by a let. It took a lot out of both players and led to three blank hands. If Hunt had given way earlier to weariness, it was Jonah's turn now to show signs of fatigue as he twice hit down and conceded a penalty point.

So it was game-ball to Hunt, at 8–6. Jonah got desperate. He started to cut off the ball earlier and produced two winning volleys to make it 7–8.

Jonah: 'When he got to six he got tired again. His first burst was too much for me but when he ran into an oxygen debt he lost his control. In trying to play the same type of game, he started to make errors. It also hit him that I was coming back again. I still felt unable to take the offensive but at 6–8 I managed those two winning volleys, not a bad effort for an ultra-defensive player out of hand.'

The next point, which also went to Jonah, was controversial. Jonah hit a parallel backhander which Hunt could not get to. Geoff asked for a let, which was turned down. Then he queried the validity of an earlier shot. This second appeal was allowed. And still, he entered into a discussion (Geoff's side of it was not audible to the gallery), at the end of which referee Chris Campbell changed his mind and ruled 'no let'.

Jonah: 'This remains a mystery. A couple of times I tried to intervene to find out what was going on. I couldn't envisage being awarded the point and I couldn't make out that it was 8–8. Very pleasing but hardly fair. An unfortunate decision. Geoff became slightly intemperate and condemned himself to death by firing into the tin while not under pressure. It cost him the match.'

Geoff lost his cool and petulantly hit the tin twice to give away the game. In the light of Jonah's loss of control in the fourth game, Geoff must now bitterly regret his failure to compose himself.

In the fourth game, Barrington repeatedly failed to keep his lob within bounds. It was self-discipline that kept him going for 21 minutes through a game in which he looked more tired than I have ever seen him before.

There were no signs of revival while Hunt climbed up to 6–0. The match looked heading for a dreadful anticlimax when Jonah suddenly came to life and beat Geoff with a fierce passing volley. Both pairs of legs were getting heavier and slower. There was a penalty point on each side during three blank hands that followed.

Jonah: 'Hunt had been 2–1 down and was now 2–2, a position he had not been in for a long time and he had been used to leading 2–1 and losing the fifth. However, he had now won the fourth and had set off for the fifth with a fresh but, as it turned out, final burst of enthusiasm.

One of the most important things about the fifth game is to get two or three quick points at the start. On most occasions, I have tended to break away but this time he did.

At six, I managed to draw out the rallies and calamity struck him in the form of tiredness. Despite the score, I was well aware that the match could still come my way but the situation called for more positive action.

Like a rat in a trap, I came out fighting, a position in which the rat's escape depends on whether he can control his fire and fury effectively. In the World Amateur final, the desperation was there but without intelligent application. Here, the brain was working ruthlessly and as my morale went up, his went down. He just died.'

Geoff was only three points from victory, but the nearness of it was not potent enough tonic to revive him for the final effort. The numbness of fatigue set in and the racket head began to droop as he addressed the ball. If he served again and took one more point, it was because Jonah hit a forcing shot into the tin and then ballooned a lob.

Jonah encountered little resistance as, in breathless silence, he went from 4–7 to 7–all. Geoff could not now get in front and Jonah finished off the match with two winning volleys.

* * * * *

AFTERMATH

Clive Everton

Three days after the Open final, Jonah slumped gloomily in my office going through a few accumulated minutiae which demanded his attention. His teeth were hurting, his gums were swollen, his face was long. He was in the throes of a colossal depression.

'You've had no match play. You've had all this trouble with your teeth. You had this stomach bug. And you won. I think that's fantastic.'

Jonah hardly flickered. He was prepared to concede that he would have felt even worse if he had lost but winning had given him no joy. At the back of it was a deep dissatisfaction that he had been forced to use a relatively negative game to win, a personal recession in that all the work he had expended on the more positive aspects of the game had been almost irrelevant. He had won but he had won infinitely less well than he wanted to win.

It was no surprise when he lost in straight games to Hunt in the Stockton-on-Tees final that weekend. Mentally, there was nothing left and physically he was dominated by the discomfort of the infection at the base of his wisdom teeth. The following Friday, he had them removed, showing one flash of spirit just previously by challenging Hunt (via Crawford White *Daily Express* interview) to another 15-match series and another by repeating the challenge, from a prone position in the Calthorpe Nursing Home, to David Davies of the *Birmingham Post*.

Thus ended Jonah's 1971–2 season, a time at which, professionally, we decided to part. He was guaranteed a basic income from contracts; I myself, with certain other interests demanding more of my time, felt the time required for organising his non-contractual activities was disproportionate to the return from any fair percentage of the fees; Madeline was bringing about some much needed tightening up in the conduct of his day to day affairs; and most of all there was a common feeling that life was too short to mount complex promotions when a more satisfactory net return could be obtained from him taking part in promotions set up by others. When Jonah is no longer a top player, a day which Jonah refuses to contemplate, he may well become a great squash entrepreneur as well as, without doubt, a writer and commentator.

But prediction, where Jonah is concerned, seems a particularly idle pastime. I cannot visualise him as part of any organisation in which he is not the boss—he has to be No 1 within the system or totally rebellious to it from outside.

'Why do so many people hate me?' he once asked, not seeking reassurance, which is something he never does though he may welcome it when it is offered, but in a spirit of genuine enquiry. Unquestionably, many people dislike him and a few do indeed hate him. Some of this can be straightforwardly attributed to envy, some to the characteristic Establishment fear of looking foolish or out of date, a fault to which the S.R.A. hierarchy has on many occasions generously subscribed.

More subtly, Jonah is disliked by people whose psychology is radically different from his own. 'Ordinary' middle-class people, when actually confronted with them and not observing their professional persona at some safe remove, rather suspect actors, painters, pop stars or sportsmen: these people do not generally have middle-class values; they are not stable; they are not 'sound'.

Artists do not behave like bank managers, stars do not behave like nonentities. Becoming a star is a competitive business, a matter not only of winning on the court but commanding the limelight through force of personality. In doing so, he offends the slightly less or much less talented who teel how nice it would be for they themselves to be the centre of the scene. Some of these (like officials and club secretaries) who realise that this cannot be achieved directly subdue their frustrations in obstruction; others still, absorbed in tiny obsessions, cannot recognise the pettiness of their own preoccupations. If Jonah's co-operation is required and he manifests less than 100% enthusiasm then the word immediately goes about that he is egotistical, unco-operative, unreliable and generally not very nice to know.

Ironically, his very desire to be obliging frequently makes him enemies. Requests for newspaper or recorded radio interviews have been made, accepted and, in the light of suddenly changing circumstances, changed, sometimes several times. He once cried off through injury a visit to Sweden for which he had agreed to charge no fee but take only his expenses. The vilification received from several quarters over that at least made him resolve never to agree to do anything free.

As with many sportsmen accustomed to planning their days exclusively around themselves, punctuality (when unconcerned with squash) is not his long suit. He holds world records for continuous occupancy of the bathroom and loo and is congenitally incapable of bringing an interesting conversation to a close when the time draws nigh for his next engagement several miles away.

Profoundly irritating as he can therefore be in small ways, he redeems all by a basic goodness of heart.

He is, at all times, his own man, not merely in pursuing his ambition but in living by values in which he believes. He has an instinctive sympathy for the underdog, bottomless contempt for pretension, an immense respect for any achievement founded on personal endeavour. He has a keen discernment of human motive, a clear perception of human wickedness, an unblinking self-knowledge, above all, a sustaining sense of humour. When the history of squash comes to be written, he will be the central character, the agent of change; the harbinger of a new order.

More immediately and perhaps more important he represents the aspiration to be better, not just the best, but outstandingly the best, not merely outstandingly the best but the best there has ever been. To remain such an entirely likable human being under that kind of burden is perhaps the most remarkable thing about him.

Barrington Match Results

1–11 January 1965—Amateur Championship Eliminating competition. 1st round: J. Barrington beat H. B. Derbyshire 9–3 5–9 9–3 9–7. 2nd round: J. Barrington beat A. H. H. Duder 9–4 7–9 10–8 9–4.
Competition Proper. 1st round: J. Barrington beat J. L. Moore (Australia) 9–5 9–4 0–9 9–6. 2nd round: S. Afifi (U.A.R.) beat J. Barrington 9–7 9–7 9–2.
South Western Area County Championships. Gloucestershire beat Cornwall 4–1 at Torquay. H. G. MacIntosh (1st string) beat J. Barrington 9–3 1–9 10–8 9–6.
Inter-county Plate Competition. Hampshire beat Cornwall 5–0 at Bournemouth. J. D. Ward (1st string) beat J. Barrington 9–1 9–4 9–1.
5, 6 and 7 March 1965. North of England Championships at Manchester. 2nd round: J. Barrington beat D. H. Shaw 9–1 10–8 0–9 9–7. 3rd round: A. M. H. Hill beat J. Barrington 9–5 9–10 6–9 10–8 9–7.
East of England Championships. 1st round: J. Barrington beat D. M. Reeve 3–0. 2nd round: J. Barrington beat J. Woods 4–9 9–6 9–5 9–3. 3rd round: J. Barrington beat K. Davidson 7–9 10–8 10–8 9–6. 4th round: J. D. Ward beat J. Barrington 9–4 9–6 3–9 9–2.
West of England Championships at Exeter. Final: Sharif Khan beat J. Barrington 3–2.
Bude Invitation Tournament 30 and 31 January 1965. Quarter-finals: J. Barrington beat B. Rowlands 9–6 9–5 8–9 9–6. Semi-finals: J. Barrington beat R. A. Lane 9–2 9–2 9–2. Final: J. Barrington beat N. Barrington 9–1 9–7 9–1.
Isle of Wight Championship 9–11 April 1965. Quarter-finals: T. D. Gathercole beat J. Barrington 1–9 10–8 1–9 9–7 9–3.
Open Championship 16–22 December 1965. 1st round: J. Barrington beat D. B. Hughes 9–5 9–2 9–7. 2nd round: T. Shafik beat J. Barrington 9–6 9–6 9–6.
South of England Championships 1965. 1st round: J. Barrington beat B. L. Ellis 9–8 9–7 9–2. 2nd round: J. Barrington beat D. White 9–6 9–7 9–8. 3rd round: J. Barrington beat D. Lock 9–1 9–6 9–2. Semi-final: J. Barrington beat Sharif Khan 9–1 9–6 0–9 9–7. Final: J. Barrington beat J. D. Ward 9–7 9–0 10–8.
Midlands Championship at Coventry, *1965.* 1st round: J. Barrington beat J. B. Smith 9–3 4–9 3–9 9–2 9–6. 2nd round: J. Barrington beat R. Harris 9–5 4–9 9–3 9–8. 3rd round: A. M. H. Hill beat J. Barrington 9–3 9–6 7–9 9–6.

Amateur Championships 7–17 January 1966. 1st round: R. M. H. Boddington beat J. Barrington 9–1 9–7 9–2.
Plate Competition. Preliminary round: J. Barrington w/o P. G. Goodwin. 1st round: N. J. Faulks beat J. Barrington 4–9 9–5 9–0 retired.
England v Ireland at R.A.C. Club, London, *1966.* England won 5–0. J. G. A. Lyon (1st string) beat J. Barrington 9–3 8–10 4–9 9–5 9–3.
Scotland v Ireland at Dublin, *1966.* Scotland won 4–1. O. L. Balfour (1st string) beat J. Barrington 9–7 9–3 10–9.
Ireland v Wales at Dublin, *1966.* Ireland won 4–1. J. Barrington (1st string) beat P. Stokes 9–2 10–8 7–9 9–6.
South Western Area County Championships 1966. Semi-finals: Dorset beat Cornwall 4–1. O. R. Stansfield (1st string) lost to J. Barrington 1–9 2–9 2–9.
North of England Championships 1966. 2nd round: J. Barrington beat M. R. Grundy 9–7 9–3 9–4. Quarter-finals: J. Barrington beat K. S. Davidson 9–3 9–5 9–1. Semi-finals: J. Barrington beat A. Ispanani 9–1 9–2 9–6. Final: J. Barrington beat Sharif Khan 7–9 9–4 9–5 10–9.
West of England Championships 1966. 2nd round: J. Barrington beat Gulmast Khan 9–1 9–0 8–9 9–5. 3rd round: J. Barrington beat A. M. H. Hill 9–3 9–3 9–3. Semi-final: J. Barrington beat T. C. Francis 9–5 9–3 9–2. Final: J. Barrington beat Sharif Khan 9–6 9–7 9–7.
Isle of Wight Championship 1–3 April 1966. Quarter-final: J. Barrington beat J. F. Skinner 9–4 9–5 9–4. Semi-final: J. Barrington beat J. D. Ward 5–9 9–3 9–2 9–1. Final: J. Barrington beat T. D. Gathercole 9–1 9–7 9–5.
Open Championships 12–21 December 1966. 1st round: J. Barrington beat M. W. Corby 9–5 7–9 9–7 9–4. 2nd round: J. Barrington beat A. Taleb 9–4 9–1 8–10 9–5. Semi-final: J. Barrington beat I. Amin 9–4 4–9 9–5 9–3. Final: J. Barrington beat A. Jawaid 9–2 6–9 9–2 9–2.
Amateur Championship 6–16 January 1967. 1st round: J. Barrington beat R. Dolman 9–4 9–5 9–4. 2nd round: J. Barrington beat P. Millman 9–5 9–2 9–5. 3rd round: J. Barrington beat H. MacIntosh 9–7 9–6 9–0. Quarter-finals: J. Barrington beat J. D. Ward 9–5 9–3 2–0 retired. Semi-final: J. Barrington beat K. Hiscoe 5–9 2–9 9–5 9–5 9–1. Final: J. Barrington beat R. Carter 1–9 9–6 7–9 9–7 9–0.
England v Ireland at Dublin, *1967.* England won 4–1. M. W. Corby (1st string) lost to J. Barrington 1–9 9–2 9–6 6–9 6–9.
Scotland v Ireland at Edinburgh, *1967.* Scotland won 3–2. O. L. Balfour (1st string) lost to J. Barrington 3–9 4–9 2–9.
Wales v Ireland at Cardiff, *1967.* Wales won 4–1. D B. Hughes (1st string) lost to J. Barrington 1–9 9–6 4–9 5–9.
South-Western Area County Championship 1967. 1st round: Cornwall beat Somerset 3–2. J. Barrington (1st string) beat C. W. Hannam 9–1 9–0 9–3. Semi-final: Cornwall beat Dorset 4–1. J. Barrington (1st string) beat O. R. Stansfield 9–1 9–3 9–6. Final: Devon beat Cornwall 3–2. M. D. Thurgur (1st string) lost to J. Barrington 1–9 6–9 7–9.
East of England Championship at Bedford, *1967.* 2nd round: J. Barrington beat D. Williams 9–7 9–5 9–2. Semi-final: J. Barrington beat B. J. Wise 9–1

7–9 9–2 9–1. Final: J. Barrington beat M. W. Corby 9–7 9–2 3–9 3–9 9–2.

Bude and North Cornwall Invitation Tournament 27–29 January 1967. Quarter-final: J. Barrington beat R. Harris 9–2 9–2 9–1. Semi-final: J. Barrington beat M. D. Thurgur 10–8 7–9 9–0 9–2. Final: J. Barrington w/o J. N. H. Smith.

International Championship Team Event at Sydney, *August 1967.* Great Britain beat South Africa 2–1. J. Barrington (1st string) beat D. Botha 9–3 9–2 9–3. Great Britain lost to Australia 0–3. J. Barrington (1st string) lost to K. Hiscoe 9–6 9–1 3–9 1–9 6–9. Great Britain beat Pakistan 3–0. J. Barrington (1st string) beat M. Saleem 9–1 9–1 9–3. Great Britain lost to New Zealand 1–2. J. Barrington (1st string) beat C. Waugh 9–4 9–0 9–4. Individual Event: Quarter-final: J. Barrington beat D. Botha 9–7 10–9 9–1. Semi-final: C. Nancarrow beat J. Barrington 9–7 9–6 9–7.

Open Championship 14–20 December 1967. 1st round: J. Barrington beat A. M. H. Hill 9–7 9–3 9–5. 2nd round: J. Barrington beat D. Brazier 9–2 9–7 9–5. Semi-finals: J. Barrington beat K. Zaghloul 9–2 9–2 9–0. Final: J. Barrington beat A. Taleb 9–6 9–0 9–5.

Amateur Championship 5–15 January 1968. 1st round: J. Barrington beat J. S. W. Hunt 9–3 9–5 9–0. 2nd round: J. Barrington beat R. A. G. White 9–2 9–2 9–2. 3rd round: J. Barrington beat B. Liebenburg 9–5 9–0 9–3. Quarter-final: J. Barrington beat D. B. Hughes 9–6 9–5 9–1. Semi-final: J. Barrington beat A. M. H. Hill 9–1 9–2 9–0. Final: J. Barrington beat M. W. Corby 9–3 9–6 2–9 9–5.

England v Ireland at Croxley Green, Herts, *1968.* England won 4–1. M. W. Corby (1st string) lost to J. Barrington 9–7 2–9 5–9 0–9.

Scotland v Ireland at Belfast, *1968.* Scotland won 3–2. O. L. Belfour (1st string) lost to J. Barrington 0–9 1–9 6–9.

Ireland v Wales at Dublin, *1968.* Ireland won 3–2. J. Barrington (1st string) beat R. A. Dolman 6–9 9–1 9–0 9–7.

South West Area County Championship at Exeter, *1968.* 1st round: Cornwall beat Dorset 4–1. J. Barrington (1st string) beat D. R. W. Potter 9–1 9–5 9–0. Semi-final: Cornwall beat Gloucester 4–1. J. Barrington (1st string) beat P. E. Millman 9–7 9–2 9–1. Final: Devon beat Cornwall 3–2. M. D. Thurgur (1st string) lost to J. Barrington 1–9 2–9 2–9.

Bude and North Cornwall Invitation Tournament 1968. Quarter-final: J. Barrington beat R. J. Harris 9–4 9–2 9–2. Semi-final: J. Barrington beat N. J. Barrington 8–10 9–3 9–5 9–3. Final: J. Barrington beat M. D. Thurgur 9–1 9–0 9–3.

Amateur Championship 6–16 December 1968. 1st round: J. Barrington beat N. J. Barrington 7–9 9–4 9–4 9–6. 2nd round: J. Barrington beat P. E. Goodwin 9–7 9–4 9–3. 3rd round: J. Barrington beat S. A. Ispahani 9–2 9–1 9–6. Quarter-final: J. Barrington beat J. D. Ward 7–9 10–8 9–7 9–1. Semi-final: J. Barrington beat P. Millman 9–4 9–0 9–0. Final: J. Barrington beat M. W. Corby 3–9 9–1 9–2 9–3.

Open Championship at Sheffield, *1968.* 1st round: J. Barrington beat K. S. Davidson 9–1 9–0 9–2. 2nd round: J. Barrington beat R. N. Lewis 9–1

9–2 9–3. Quarter-final: J. Barrington beat A. M. H. Hill 9–3 9–4 9–2. Semi-final: C. Nancarrow beat J. Barrington 9–4 9–5 10–8.

2nd International Championship February 1969. Great Britain beat U.A.R. 2–1 at Malvern. J. Barrington (1st string) beat S. Afifi 9–5 9–1 9–6. Great Britain beat New Zealand 2–1 at Birmingham. J. Barrington (1st string) beat T. Johnston 9–4 9–0 9–3. Great Britain beat South Africa 3–0 at Birmingham. J. Barrington beat D. Botha 9–4 9–0 9–3. Great Britain beat Pakistan 2–1 at Nottingham. J. Barrington (1st string) beat A. Jawaid 2–9 9–5 4–9 9–3 10–8. Great Britain lost to Australia 1–2 at Birmingham. J. Barrington (1st string) beat G. Hunt 2–9 9–4 8–10 9–4 9–7. Individual event: 1st round: J. Barrington beat D Botha 9–0 9–5 9–4. 2nd round: J. Barrington beat P. Dibley 9–2 9–1 9–2. 3rd round: J. Barrington beat P. Kirton 9–1 9–0 9–3. Quarter-final: J. Barrington beat T. Johnston 9–7 9–1 9–2. Semi-final: J. Barrington beat C. Nancarrow 9–0 9–2 10–8. Final: G. Hunt beat J. Barrington 9–7 2–9 9–4 9–0.

England v Ireland at Belfast, *1969*. England won 4–1. M. W. Corby (1st string) lost to J. Barrington 1–9 9–3 2–9 4–9.

South West Area County Championship 10–12 January 1969 at Taunton. Semi-final: Devon beat Cornwall 3–2. M. D. Thurgur (1st string) lost to J. Barrington 0–9 0–9 4–9.

Bude and North Cornwall Open Invitation 15 and 16 March 1969. Semi-final: J. Barrington beat N. J. Barrington 9–3 9–3 9–3. Final: J. Barrington beat M. D. Thurgur 7–9 9–6 9–4 9–7.

Open Championship at Birmingham, *1969*. 1st round: J. Barrington beat D. M. Innes 7–9 9–4 9–7 9–1. 2nd round: J. Barrington beat J. N. C. Easter 9–6 9–1 9–4. Semi-final: J. Barrington beat M. Yasin 9–5 6–9 9–5 9–3. Final: J. Barrington beat G. Hunt 9–7 3–9 3–9 9–4 9–4.

South West Area County Championship 1970. 1st round: Devon beat Cornwall 3–2. M. D. Thurgur (1st string) lost to J. Barrington 9–4 4–9 2–9 9–5 8–10.

Open Championship at Birmingham, *4–12 December 1970*. 2nd round: J. Barrington beat G. Alauddin 9–4 9–0 9–0. 3rd round: J. Barrington beat T. C. Francis 9–0 9–0 9–2. Quarter-final: J. Barrington beat M. Z. Hepker 9–2 9–1 9–0. Semi-final: J. Barrington beat Sharif Khan 9–0 9–7 3–9 9–3. Final: J. Barrington beat A. Jawaid 9–1 9–2 9–6.

South East of England Championship 1971. Quarter-final: J. Barrington beat G. Alauddin 9–3 retired. Semi-final: J. Barrington beat R. Ratinac 9–2 9–1 4–9 9–4. Final: J. Barrington beat C. Nancarrow 6–9 4–9 9–6 9–0 9–3.

North West Open Tournament 11–17 January 1971. Quarter-final: J. Barrington beat A. Nadi 9–1 9–3 9–1. Semi-final: J. Barrington beat C. Nancarrow 9–7 9–7 9–0. Final: J. Barrington beat A. Jawaid 9–3 9–4 9–1.

Stockton-on-Tees Open Tournament 19–21 February 1971. Quarter-final: J. Barrington beat B. Patterson 9–1 9–0 9–0. Semi-final: J. Barrington beat T. Francis 9–3 9–2 9–4. Final: J. Barrington beat A. Taleb 9–3 9–2 9–7.

Index

Compiled by F. D. Buck